THOMAS JEFFERSON

and the

VIRGINIA STATUTE FOR

RELIGIOUS FREEDOM

Faith & Liberty in Fredericksburg

MICHAEL AUBRECHT

THE
History
PRESS

Published by The History Press
Charleston, SC
www.historypress.com

Copyright © 2024 by *Michael Aubrecht*
All rights reserved

Front inlay: Thomas Jefferson, by Rembrandt Peale. *White House Collection/White House Historical Association.*
Front, bottom: Fredericksburg from Falmouth, by Alfred A. Waud. *Library of Congress.*

First published 2024

Manufactured in the United States

ISBN 9781467156585

Library of Congress Control Number: 2023950473

I am for freedom of religion, and against all maneuvers to bring about a legal ascendancy of one sect over another.

—Thomas Jefferson to Elbridge Gerry, 1799

CONTENTS

CONTENTS

FOREWORD

Michael Aubrecht is a self-made scholar. Hailing from western Pennsylvania, Aubrecht and his family found themselves moving to Fredericksburg for work purposes. It is there that he became passionate about U.S. history like never before. In Fredericksburg, he found much to love and learn. Virginia history became Aubrecht's calling, and it wasn't long before he was engaged in local battlefields and churches and the historical richness they have to offer.

Aubrecht, an enthusiast, rapidly became an expert in Civil War and local church history. Always a talented writer, it wasn't long before interest and expertise turned into action. Aubrecht has since written and published several books, magazine articles, and produced an outstanding and celebrated documentary. He achieved all of this without any formal academic training in history or historical writing. It is impressive.

In his newest work, Aubrecht has taken on a much more difficult task: writing something new about Thomas Jefferson. He asked: What was Thomas Jefferson thinking about religious freedom when he wrote the Virginia statute? Is there anything that we can glean from his discourse with others and from his local involvements? Aubrecht started with what he knew and built his work from his expertise in Fredericksburg history. The result was that there is much more to learn looking through the lens of local interactions and social discourse. Aubrecht presents the reader with new information and a new perspective through the use of primary materials underused in previous works. He provides evidence and discourse that intrigues and informs. Jefferson was clearly against the establishment of any single religion supported by the government and against any power given to any body politic to inhibit religious freedom.

The story isn't a new one, but the evidence and analysis provided in Aubrecht's work adds to what anthropologist Clifford Geertz described as "thick description." Geertz's ethnographic method demanded that researchers immerse themselves in a specific culture, focusing on the social actions and behaviors of the participants. Applied to history, this requires not only noting what historical actors did but understanding why they did it, what they were thinking and how they talked/wrote about it. The strength of Aubrecht's work is that it sheds light on the social discourse and interactions surrounding the foundational law for the establishment of religious freedom in America. Aubrecht shows primary evidence, full and complete writings of historical actors and how all of this history is remembered and memorialized.

The result is twofold: a better understanding of what informed historical actors, mainly Jefferson, and the laws they established and a better understanding of how the history of the statute was and is remembered. There is no doubt that there is an ongoing historical and political discussion about what Jefferson and all of the forefathers intended regarding the role of religion in America. In this effort, Aubrecht uses local and national sources to broaden the historical understanding of the history of religious freedom and its roots in Fredericksburg, Virginia.

Maroon A. David III
Historian
United States, cultural and environmental

ACKNOWLEDGEMENTS

It's been fifteen years since my last book with The History Press was published, and it's been fifteen years since I've had the idea for this book. Being an avid scholar of Thomas Jefferson (maybe obsessed is more like it) and a Fredericksburg, Virginia resident, it wasn't a far stretch to feel qualified to tackle this subject matter. I had been feeling the itch to get back in the writer's chair, and this topic jumped back into my mind before I even got comfortable. I had a wonderful experience with the good folks at The History Press, so I sent them a short note on their website pitching the idea, just to test the waters. Kate Jenkins, an acquisitions editor, got back to me right away, and we discussed the premise of the book and what I envisioned. Kate immediately "got it" and was instrumental in helping this project come to fruition.

   The subject of Thomas Jefferson's experiences in Fredericksburg and the roots leading up to the Virginia Statute for Religious Freedom had not been examined definitively in any single study—at least from the angle at which I am pursuing it. In 1998, Cambridge Studies in Religion and American Public Life Series included a book titled *The Virginia Statute for Religious Freedom: Its Evolution and Consequences in American History*, but as this book looks at the statute from more of a political and sociological perspective, my study is more regional. Author Steven Waldman has also published a broad examination titled *Founding Faith: Providence, Politics, and the Birth of Religious Freedom in America*, but once again, my focus is on the local experience and influence on the birth of the document.

ACKNOWLEDGEMENTS

Thomas Jefferson's signature. *Wikipedia*.

As with all historical studies, this book required a lot of research. As soon as the book got the green light, I reached out to every source that came to mind. This included the University of Mary Washington, Virginia Museum of History and Culture, Rappahannock Colonial Heritage Society, Rappahannock Library, the *Free Lance-Star*, Dovetail Cultural Resource Group, City of Fredericksburg, the National Archives online and, of course, the good people at Monticello. Every one of them got back to me within a day and were more than happy to assist me in my search. Andi Russell, Jonas Beals, John Reifenberg, Paul "Trip" Wiggins, Angie Kemp, Matthew Guillen, Peter G. Mangle, Nancy Moore, Kerri Barile and Kate Schwartz could not have been more accommodating, and their assistance was vital to telling this story.

For me, it's the research that gives me the thrill. The writing is the result. Looking through archives and libraries of overlooked or unpublished material is why I'm a historian. With a subject like Thomas Jefferson, there is a lot of material that is not new. But pairing him with the subject of Fredericksburg and how it relates to the Virginia Statute for Religious Freedom is where the originality lies. No one has tried to do a definitive study from that angle—hence my idea. When I was first looking at approaching this subject, I wasn't sure if there would be enough reference material from which to draw. Once I started down the rabbit hole, I found a plethora of information. I remember thinking to myself, "Why hasn't anyone done this before?"

Once I had a rough draft of the manuscript, I did what I do with all of my books. I sent it to my personal editor, who also happens to be my father, Thomas Aubrecht. He's edited all of my manuscripts, and his work is exemplary. The quality of my other two books with The History Press are due much in part to his keen eye. My mother, Linda Aubrecht, doesn't see him very much during this time. Assembling the images is always fun for me. I love the research involved with finding pictures and deciding where they most effectively fit within the copy. This book is a blend of both period and modern imagery. The locations for these came from printed and online sources. Finding the originator and getting permission to reprint some of them was a bit of a challenge.

After I had a finished manuscript and image gallery, it was off to the editors at The History Press. Copy Editor Ashley Hill did an outstanding job making sure my writing was as clean as it can be.

I am very fortunate to have my lifelong friend and fellow historian Maroon David write the foreword to the book. He has taught me so much about being a historian, and for that, I am eternally grateful.

Of course, I have to thank the most important part of this project and any project, my family. They bear the brunt of my work. They have to deal with my absence when I'm off conducting research and my unavailability when I'm busy writing and editing. To Tracy, Dylan, Madison, Kierstyn, Jackson and, our newest addition, my grandson, Eli, your love and support means more than I can express with the written word.

INTRODUCTION

As with my previous books published by The History Press, I have labored through what I consider to be considerable research to bring to light a far too overlooked moment in time that took place in the history of Fredericksburg. My first The History Press book, *Historic Churches of Fredericksburg: Houses of the Holy*, told the story of the five historic churches in the city before, during and after the Civil War. The second, *The Civil War in Spotsylvania County: Confederate Campfires at the Crossroads*, told the story of the southern solders' lives on and off the battlefield while in the adjacent county. Both of these books explored subjects that had not been covered before—at least not in the way I covered them.

My relationship with Thomas Jefferson began as a child on a family trip to Monticello. I remember being captivated by what I saw and heard. As I became an adult—and especially as a historian—Jefferson became a bit of an obsession. The complexity of the man fascinates me. Is he a hero? Not to me. I recognize his flaws just as I recognize his contributions. That is what makes him so interesting. He was a man who did so many extraordinary things, but he is also guilty of committing some undefendable things. In the end, Jefferson is human, not some faultless patriotic idol, as he is so often portrayed.

Referred to as one of the country's most historic cities, the town of Fredericksburg is steeped in eighteenth- and nineteenth-century historic events. Historians have done an extremely good job commemorating the Battle of Fredericksburg (clearly the city's marquee event) in many books, but

I am not aware of any that have focused specifically on Thomas Jefferson's time in Fredericksburg in 1777, when he drafted the Virginia Statute for Religious Freedom.

I was surprised at the amount of reference material I was able to compile from multiple sources. The test was to know where to look. In addition to the aforementioned sources, Thomas E. Buckley's *Establishing Religious Freedom: Jefferson's Statute in Virginia* was a great reference, albeit not the easiest read. I was also able to use multiple online sources, including the National Archive's Founders Online and the *Thomas Jefferson Encyclopedia* online at Monticello.

You will note this book contains two significant themes: Thomas Jefferson in relation to the City of Fredericksburg and the result of his drafting of the Statute of Virginia for Religious Freedom, now more commonly known as the Virginia Statute for Religious Freedom. You will also see that this book is filled with many letters from Jefferson regarding the city and his statute. This is because I wanted this story to be reinforced by the words of the man himself. My goal with a book of this length is to give you a glimpse into this far too overlooked and neglected story. It is my hope that this book will not only be a pleasurable read but also become a reference for the next historian who tackles this subject. I have also included a list of historical sites in the City of Fredericksburg that are related to this story (see appendix E). This will be a valuable resource for those who are interested in following in the footsteps of this story's participants. Let's begin.

Prior to his death, Thomas Jefferson left behind specific instructions for the obelisk monument that was to mark his grave. In addition to sketching out the exact size and shape of the stone, he requested:

The following would be to my Manes the most gratifying.
On the grave
a plain die or cube of 3. f. without any mouldings, surmounted by an Obelisk of 6. f. height, each of a single stone: on the faces of the Obelisk the following inscription, & not a word more
Here was buried
Thomas Jefferson
Author of the Declaration of American Independence
of the Statute of Virginia for Religious Freedom
& Father of the University of Virginia.
because by these, as testimonials that I have lived, I wish most to be remembered. to be of the coarse stone of which my columns are made, that no one might be tempted hereafter to destroy it for the value of the materials.

*my bust by Ceracchi, with the pedestal and truncated column on which it
stands, might be given to the University if they would place it in the Dome
room of the Rotunda. On the Die of the obelisk might be engraved
Born Apr. 2. 1743. O. S.
Died —*

These contributions were, in his words, the "testimonials that I have lived,
I wish most to be remembered." It is curious that with all his contributions,
such as the political offices he held (president of the United States being
one), he selected these three specific memories. Author of the Declaration
of American Independence is obvious. Father of the University of Virginia
is understandable. But the astonishing choice is the author of the Virginia
Statute for Religious Freedom. It's not that this is unimportant, but of all his
achievements, this one is often overlooked.

Jefferson crafted this statute not in Philadelphia or one of the other busy
cities of the day. He wrote it while staying in a small Virginia town on the
Rappahannock River called Fredericksburg. Jefferson often passed through
the town on his journeys to and from Monticello. Jefferson was a second
cousin of Ann Randolph Fitzhugh and a good friend of William Fitzhugh,
the builders of one of the town's largest estates called Chatham.

Thomas Jefferson's gravesite at
Monticello. *Michael Aubrecht.*

In 1777, Jefferson stayed at Weedon's Tavern (then called Smith's) in Fredericksburg, where he penned the actual life-altering document. It established the right of every man and woman to their own religious beliefs and opinions. The Virginia General Assembly passed the landmark statute in 1786, and in 1791, it became the basis for the First Amendment to the U.S. Constitution.

The event not only had a lasting effect on the country, but it more specifically had a permanent effect on the city where the proposition was written. In 1932, the Fredericksburg City Council commissioned St. Clair Brooks, a stonemason, to erect a monument commemorating Jefferson's bill. It is built from stones sent from churches across the country. Each January, the Religious Freedom Day parade hits the streets of downtown Fredericksburg to commemorate the anniversary of Jefferson drafting the statute.

However, the story of Jefferson's experiences in Fredericksburg and drafting the Virginia Statute for Religious Freedom is much more than just a memorial and parade.

1

THOMAS JEFFERSON

I prefer dangerous freedom over peaceful slavery.
—*Thomas Jefferson*

Born in Albemarle County, Virginia, in April 1743, Thomas Jefferson's original intention was to study the principles of law at the College of William and Mary and become an attorney. During this period, he also developed an intense interest in both science and philosophy. With apparent literary and diplomatic skills, Jefferson also showed an early aptitude for politics. As a delegate to the Continental Congress, he drafted the Declaration of Independence. In 1776, he entered the Virginia House of Delegates and initiated a comprehensive reform program for the abolition of feudal survivals in land tenure and the separation of church and state. Reform and limited government were mainstays in Jefferson's dogma through the years.

His list of political positions held is staggering and include: member of the Virginia House of Burgesses, county lieutenant, county surveyor, deputy delegate of the Second Continental Congress, member of the Virginia House of Delegates, governor of Virginia, delegate to Congress, commissioner to France, minister to France, secretary of state and vice president and president of the United States. He was the third American president and the first to be inaugurated in Washington, D.C.

As a Democratic-Republican, Jefferson's most notable achievement while in office was the purchase of the Louisiana Territory from France in 1803. In retrospect, the weighty transaction was surely in violation of his earlier

Jefferson portrait by Charles Willson Peale, 1791. *Worldhistory.org.*

constitutional scruples, and although it significantly expanded the nation's acreage, the question remained about whether the government had a right to buy it in the first place. Reelected in 1804, Jefferson tried desperately to keep the United States out of the Napoleonic Wars in Europe, employing, to this end, the unpopular embargo policy.

Over the course of his life, Jefferson was a prolific writer and thinker who authored various works on politics, history, science and philosophy. Some of his most prominent written works include:

A Summary View of the Rights of British America (1774)
Declaration of the Causes and Necessity of Taking Up Arms (1775)
Declaration of Independence (1776)
Virginia Statute for Religious Freedom (1777)
Notes on the State of Virginia (1785)
Manual of Parliamentary Practice for the Use of the Senate of the United
*   States (1801)*
The Life and Morals of Jesus of Nazareth (1819)
The Thomas Jefferson Papers (1606–1826)

Jefferson wrote only one full-length book, *Notes on the State of Virginia*. In it, he attacked the tyranny of the church. According to the *Thomas Jefferson Encyclopedia*:

> *Equally controversial were Jefferson's statements on religious freedom. In Query XVII: "Religion," he defended a separation of church and state, arguing that "it does me no injury for my neighbour to say there are twenty gods, or no god. It neither picks my pocket nor breaks my leg."*

He also wrote:

> *Difference of opinion, is advantageous in religion.*

> *That these profess probably a thousand different systems of religion. That ours is but one of that thousand. That if there be but one right, and ours that one, we should wish to see the 999 wandering sects gathered into the fold of truth.*

> *But every state, says an inquisitor, has established some religion. No two, say I, have established the same. Is this a proof of the infallibility of establishments?*

> *Our sister states of Pennsylvania and New-York, however, have long subsisted without any establishment at all. They flourish infinitely. Religion is well supported; of various kinds, indeed, but all good enough; all sufficient to preserve peace and order.*

These views were to be used against him in the heated presidential campaign of 1800, when, for example, William Linn, a leading Federalist clergyman, penned a campaign pamphlet attacking Jefferson's presumed atheism and warning voters, "Let my neighbor once persuade himself that there is no God, and he will soon pick my pocket, and break not only my leg but my neck."

Linn adamantly disparaged Jefferson because he thought he was an atheist whose views contradicted scripture. As he wrote in the introduction to the pamphlet titled *Serious Considerations on the Election of a President: Addressed to the Citizens of the United States*, "My objection to his being promoted to the Presidency is founded singly upon his disbelief of the Holy Scriptures…and open promotion of Deism." All his criticisms of Jefferson, including those regarding Native Americans and "Negroes," were essentially attacks on his religious views.

From 1797 to 1798, Jefferson and Linn conducted correspondence to discuss their shared interest in studying Native American languages. At no point during this time do the letters show any signs of disagreement. Linn mainly took exception to Jefferson's thoughts in his *Notes on the State of Virginia*.

He argued that Jefferson's comments were "repugnant to sacred history" because they implied that the Native Americans were "a distinct race of men originally created and placed in America contrary to the biblical teachings that all mankind have descended from a single pair meaning Adam and Eve."

In addition, Linn complained about Jefferson's statement that "the blacks, whether originally a distinct race, or made distinct by time and circumstances, are inferior to the whites in the endowments both of body and mind.…will not a lover of nature history then…excuse an effort to keep those in the department of man as distinct as nature has formed them?" Linn was again offended and stated, "Would a man who believes in a divine revelation even hint a suspicion of this kind?"

Linn referred to Jefferson as an infidel and insisted that Jefferson "degraded the blacks from the rank which God hath given them in the scale of being! You have advanced the strongest argument for their state of slavery! You have insulted human nature!…We exclude you, in your present belief, from any department among Christians!"

Jefferson was elected and reinforced his support of freedom of religion in his first inaugural address on March 4, 1801:

> *About to enter, fellow-citizens, on the exercise of duties which comprehend everything dear and valuable to you, it is proper you should understand what I deem the essential principles of our Government, and consequently*

those which ought to shape its Administration. I will compress them within the narrowest compass they will bear, stating the general principle, but not all its limitations. Equal and exact justice to all men, of whatever state or persuasion, religious or political; peace, commerce, and honest friendship with all nations, entangling alliances with none; the support of the State governments in all their rights, as the most competent administrations for our domestic concerns and the surest bulwarks against antirepublican tendencies; the preservation of the General Government in its whole constitutional vigor, as the sheet anchor of our peace at home and safety abroad; a jealous care of the right of election by the people—a mild and safe corrective of abuses which are lopped by the sword of revolution where peaceable remedies are unprovided; absolute acquiescence in the decisions of the majority, the vital principle of republics, from which is no appeal but to force, the vital principle and immediate parent of despotism; a well-disciplined militia, our best reliance in peace and for the first moments of war till regulars may relieve them; the supremacy of the civil over the military authority; economy in the public expense, that labor may be lightly burthened; the honest payment of our debts and sacred preservation of the public faith; encouragement of agriculture, and of commerce as its handmaid; the diffusion of information and arraignment of all abuses at the bar of the public reason; freedom of religion; freedom of the press, and freedom of person under the protection of the habeas corpus, and trial by juries impartially selected. These principles form the bright constellation which has gone before us and guided our steps through an age of revolution and reformation.

He later wrote a "Summary of Public Service" dated after September 2, 1800. In it, he stated:

[after September 2, 1800]
I have sometimes asked myself whether my country is the better for my having lived at all? I do not know that it is. I have been the instrument of doing the following things; but they would have been done by others; some of them perhaps a little later.

1776. I proposed the demolition of the church establishment, and the freedom of religion. it could only be done by degrees. towit 1776. c. 2. exempted dissenters from contributions to the church & left the church clergy to be supported by voluntary contributions of their own sect. continued from year to year & made perpetual 1779. c. 36. I prepared the act for religious

Monticello. *Colonialwilliamsburg.org.*

freedom in 1777. as part of the revisal, which was not reported to the assembly till 1779. and that particular law not passed till 1785. and then by the efforts of mr Madison.

After his retirement in 1809, Jefferson eagerly returned to his beloved estate, Monticello, where he developed an interest in education, founded the University of Virginia and watched its development with great interest. He died at Monticello on July 4, 1826, which ironically was the fiftieth anniversary of the signing of the Declaration of Independence.

Today, religion remains a hotly debated aspect of Thomas Jefferson's legacy. Some claim that he was simply a Deist, while others have accused him of having no faith at all. Jefferson would have been "officially" categorized as a reformed Protestant and was raised as an Episcopalian (Anglican). However, his tendency for wanting to possess a broader knowledge and understanding of all things led him to be influenced by English Deists, who believed in the concept that a higher power did indeed exist but that man's affairs were not under its influence.

He also held many beliefs in common with Unitarians of the period and sometimes wrote that he thought the whole country would eventually become a Unitarian society. Jefferson recorded that the teachings of Jesus contain the "outlines of a system of the most sublime morality which has ever fallen from the lips of man." He added, "I am of a sect by myself, as far as I know."

Although his specific denominational and congregational ties were limited in his adulthood and his ever-evolving theological beliefs were distinctively his own, Jefferson was, by his own admission, a progressive "Christian," if only in intent. He attended Episcopalian services as president, but his manipulation and rewriting of the Christian Bible certainly speaks to a man who was both curious and conflicted. He once wrote, "I am a Christian, in the only sense in which he wished anyone to be." This aspect of Jefferson's personal belief system remains among the most controversial and debated of all. Bible scholars have accused him of being both a genius and an atheist.

Only the former is true.

2

CITY OF FREDERICKSBURG

Fredericksburg's identity and character are directly related to its rich history.
—City of Fredericksburg website

I n order to understand the significance of the City of Fredericksburg, one must first look at the locality and the important role that organized religion played in the town. Today, the town is known as "America's Most Historic City," while the neighboring county of Spotsylvania is referred to as the "Crossroads of the Civil War." Both are saturated with landmark homesteads, museums, plantations and battlefields that draw countless tourists every year. Churches remain among some of the most coveted attractions for their historical significance and architectural beauty.

Fredericksburg has also been referred to as a "city of churches," as its silhouette is dominated by a plethora of bell towers and steepled roofs. Today, there are over three hundred congregations spread throughout the surrounding region. Clearly, anyone walking through the town can see the important role religion played in the day-to-day lives of the town's inhabitants. Chartered in 1728, the settlement served as the surrounding area's political, social and economic center. As it was conveniently located on the banks of the Rappahannock River, Fredericksburg quickly became a bustling metropolis, with taverns, lodging and commerce. Both eighteenth- and nineteenth-century industries, such as mills, shipping and transportation, helped establish the town as a commercial beacon on the ever-expanding map of central Virginia.

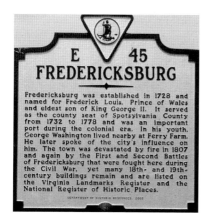

E 45
FREDERICKSBURG

Fredericksburg was established in 1728 and named for Frederick Louis, Prince of Wales and eldest son of King George II. It served as the county seat of Spotsylvania County from 1732 to 1778 and was an important port during the colonial era. In his youth, George Washington lived nearby at Ferry Farm. He later spoke of the city's influence on him. The town was devastated by fire in 1807 and again by the First and Second Battles of Fredericksburg that were fought here during the Civil War, yet many 18th- and 19th-century buildings remain and are listed on the Virginia Landmarks Register and the National Register of Historic Places.

DEPARTMENT OF HISTORIC RESOURCES. 2002

City of Fredericksburg historical marker. *Dawn Bowen.*

Despite a widespread disenchantment among America's first settlers with the Church of England, religion remained a precious keystone in colonial life. Many of the area's first citizens retained their belief in God and brought the deep desire to practice their faith with them when they came to this new land. It was the freedom to pursue that faith in a variety of forms that separated the early colonial Protestant and even Catholic churches from their European counterparts. Therefore, churches were significantly important institutions in the foundation of any settlement in the New World.

The original English settlement of Fredericksburg had been clustered in a fifty-acre area along the west bank of the river. It was originally engineered in a grid-like pattern, with wide streets that were named after British royalty. The initial plot consisted of sixty-four equally sized lots with two extra spaces for a church and a market. As the population increased, Fredericksburg found it necessary to expand the municipal boundaries. By 1759, the city had tripled its physical size, opening the door to both new merchants and settlers alike.

The most prominent church in town during the colonial period was St. George's Episcopal, which would benefit greatly from Jefferson's statute. Located at the corner of Princess Anne and George Streets, this church was built by Colonel Henry Willis in 1732. The current structure was built in 1849 and was the third church to be constructed on the premises. Colonel John Spotswood, the son of the colonial governor, donated the church's original bell in 1751. The city council placed a clock in the bell tower in 1851.

St. George's also has several rather unique distinctions that set it apart from the other congregations of Fredericksburg. Foremost, it was the first church established at the original settlement of Germanna in 1720 and was known as Saint George's Parish by the House of Burgesses of Colonial Virginia. Eight years later, the assembly formally established the City of Fredericksburg, Virginia. Therefore, St. George's is the only church in the entire city that was founded—actually, mandated—by English rule.

Along with the English Church came English rules and regulations. Many of the punishments for breaking the covenants of the church were

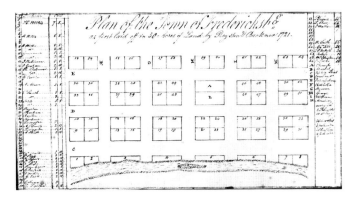

Plan of the town
of Fredericksburg,
1721. *Rappahannock
Colonial Heritage
Society.*

also bought over from England to the New World. This included public
ridicules and nonlethal tortures, which were used to enforce both civic and
congregational codes. The Act of Assembly in 1705 established a strict list
of "Religious Offenses" and appropriate punishments.

Despite its strict code of conduct and ties to England, St. George's
prospered and grew into a bustling church in early Virginia. During the
colonial period, the church was responsible for the health and welfare of
orphans, widows and the sick. It also assisted the poor and downtrodden. As
a spiritually educating pillar in the community, St. George's also established
both men's and women's charity schools.

Throughout the mid- and late 1700s, members and friends of the
Washington family begin attending services at St. George's. They included
William Paul, brother to America's father of naval warfare Commodore John
Paul Jones, as well as George Washington's brother Charles and brother-in-
law Fielding Lewis, who also served the church as a vestryman.

As the city developed, a rift remained between the citizens of the city
who found differences in social, political and spiritual aspects of life.
Slaveholding was a particularly sensitive issue, as the town's white citizens
were divided along pro- and antislavery lines. Numbers of influential white
citizens held meetings at the local churches and town hall calling for the
support of African colonization. These meetings were deemed unpopular
by many, as the institution of slavery in the Old Dominion had been in
place for generations. Traced back to the earliest colonization of America,
human bondage remained one of the most controversial aspects of the
country's culture.

For his entire life, Thomas Jefferson was surrounded by the practice of
slavery. In 1764, he inherited 20 enslaved people from his father. Ten years
later, he inherited 135 more from his father-in-law, John Wayles, who was

Saint George's Episcopal Church, Fredericksburg, Virginia. *From the* Dairy Free Traveler.

involved in the importation of enslaved Africans into Virginia. By 1796, Jefferson enslaved approximately 170 people, with 50 living on his property in Bedford County and 120 residing in Albemarle. Each residence was completely dependent on the use of forced labor, from the planting of fields to the daily operations of the house. Over 400 enslaved people lived and worked at Monticello. Close to 100 served at Poplar Forest. Enslaved labor was also the economic force behind many of Jefferson's enterprises. It seems that his lifestyle demanded the practice, regardless of his prejudices against it.

Ironically, throughout his career, both politically and personally, Jefferson repeatedly voiced displeasure with the institution of slavery. He often referred to it as an "abominable crime," a "moral depravity," a "hideous blot" and a "fatal stain" that deformed "what nature had bestowed on us of her fairest gifts." He was successful in outlawing international slave trade in the Old Dominion but continued to enslave people on all his farms in Virginia. This blatant contradiction illustrates the complexity that was Thomas Jefferson. As the author of the Declaration of Independence, which declared "all men are created equal," Jefferson did not believe this was entirely true. One conclusion is that he believed a practicable solution to this moral dilemma could not be found in his lifetime. He continued, however, to advocate privately his own emancipation plan, which included a provision for colonizing.

Jefferson's enslaved people did have the freedom to practice their religion. They would often hold formal and informal prayer meetings on weeknights in their cabins while holding more visible ceremonies outside on Sundays. Preachers licensed by the church and hired by enslavers were supplemented by enslaved preachers. There is no evidence that Jefferson hired a white preacher for his enslaved people. Texts from the Bible, which most enslaved people could not read, were explicated by verses from the spirituals. Records indicate a rich spiritual life at Monticello incorporating both European and African traditions, including Christianity. It is documented that an enslaved woodworker named John Hemmings and his wife, Priscilla, held prayer meetings in their cabin, and there is at least one reference to a baptism.

Jefferson often traveled through Fredericksburg en route to and from his estate Monticello. He frequently commented that the road from Fredericksburg "was the worst." In a letter to Charles Lewis Bankhead, Jefferson described the road from Fredericksburg:

Washington Feb. 27. 09.
Dear Sir
The inclosed [sic] *will, I presume, inform you that all are well at Edgehill.*
the family will remove to Monticello on the 9ᵗʰ. or 10ᵗʰ. of March. I am in
hopes to join them, about the 15ᵗʰ. or 16ᵗʰ. I imagine you will be in motion
by that time, the roads permitting. Would it not be better for you, instead
of going by Fredericksburg, to find the best road to Anderson's bridge on the
North Anna, which is in the direct line from Port-Royal to Monticello. from
that bridge there is a good road all along the ridge between the head waters
of the North & South Anna. the direct rout [sic] *from Portroyal would*
pass between Todd's ordinary & Mattapony church. I think this would
save you considerable distance, and give you a good road instead of the
impassable one from Fredericksburg to Monticello. Congress continues in
an indecisive state. I think they will substitute a total non-intercourse with
France & England & their territories instead of the embargo after the 4ᵗʰ.
of March. but it is impossible to pronounce on this. we must know how in
four days. be so good as to present my respects to your father & family, my
love to Anne and accept my affectionate salutations.
Th: Jefferson

In May 1766, Jefferson spent two or three days with his friends the Fitzhughs on his way to Annapolis, Maryland. This visit took place at the Somerset Plantation, since the Fitzhughs' stately home, Chatham Manor, was not completed until 1771. On August 24, 1790, Jefferson wrote to Fitzhugh, "If I go by way of Fredericksburg, I shall surely have the pleasure to call and ask how you do." In letters from August 7, 1790, and September 5, 1790, Jefferson wrote, "I shall be happy in seeing you in Chatham."

In a letter dated October 29, 1790, Jefferson repeated his earlier aim: "Should I take the route of Fredericksburg I will endeavor to have the pleasure of seeing you." In a letter to Mann Page dated December 8, 1793, Jefferson wrote:

I owe you a letter which should have been written by your servant from
Fredericksbg. [sic], *when you were so kind as to send for me when I was*
there. But I had passed the day at Chatham, was returning about dusk,
shivering, and snowing, when I met your servant in the streets.

According to the National Park Service, the probable date of Jefferson's visit was October 27, 1793, as Jefferson kept a detailed record of his

Chatham Manor. *B101.5.*

expenses. The journal entry for October 27 includes: "Ferriage, etc. Chatham $.25." At the time, Jefferson was the secretary of state. Mann Page was a friend of Jefferson and the brother of John Page, the governor of Virginia from 1802 to 1805. Page owned the Mannsfield Plantation south of Fredericksburg. Jefferson's letter indicates his plans to pass through Fredericksburg in January 1794.

In his memorandum book from 1798, Jefferson stated that he arrived in Fredericksburg on June 30 and was saluted by a local artillery.

As a man of the Age of Enlightenment, Jefferson compulsively recorded, measured and calculated the world around him. This was especially true when he traveled. Jefferson recorded his observations about the natural world he explored, jotted down details about the cities he visited and the people he encountered and kept records of the goods he bought. All the while, he kept detailed notes in his account book on the distances he crossed and the roads he traveled. Jefferson preferred to travel alone. In a letter to John Banister Jr., dated June 19, 1787, he wrote, "I think one travels more usefully when they travel alone, because they reflect more."

Despite his affinity for traveling solo, Jefferson had friends he visited along the way. The Fitzhughs lived a lavish life that included experimental farming and horse racing.

Left: Ann Randolph Fitzhugh. *Right*: William Fitzhugh. *Colonial Virginia Portraits.*

As the son of a prosperous Virginia family, William was born in 1741, the only son of Henry and Lucy Carter Fitzhugh. His father died before William's second birthday, leaving him the heir of a vast family fortune. On April 2, 1763, Fitzhugh married another prominent Virginian, Ann Randolph. After their wedding, they lived at Somerset, one of two plantations Fitzhugh had inherited by 1765. Desiring a larger residence, the couple sold nine thousand acres of land in Spotsylvania County to finance the building of another home, this one on the banks of the Rappahannock River overlooking the City of Fredericksburg.

Like his friend Jefferson, Fitzhugh was also heavily involved in politics. He put his name up for election to the House of Burgesses, serving between 1772 and 1775. When the assembly was dissolved by Lord Dunmore, Fitzhugh continued to serve King George County in ad hoc conventions held in Williamsburg and Richmond. He was also a member of the Revolutionary Committee of Safety at this time (1774–75). Fitzhugh supported the Revolution wholeheartedly. During the war, he acted as a commissioner of two arms and munitions factories in the area, while also serving as a member of the Virginia House of Delegates (1776–77) and later as a state senator (1780–87).

Fredericksburg is also the site of many other noteworthy locations from the time of Jefferson. In 1738, George Washington's family moved to Ferry

George Washington
portrait by Stuart
Gilbert, circa 1900–
1912. *Library of Congress.*

Farm, then known simply as the Washington Farm, near the Rappahannock River, opposite Fredericksburg. His mother, Mary Ball Washington, moved to a house in the heart of the city after taking care of the farm became too cumbersome. George's sister Betty lived at Kenmore, a plantation house on the edge of town. In the 1770s, Betty's husband, Fielding Lewis, and Washington operated an arms factory for the Continental Army. Revolutionary War generals George Weedon and Hugh Mercer lived in Fredericksburg along with naval captain John Paul Jones. Future U.S. president James Monroe lived and practiced law in the city.

Fredericksburg has more than 270 original eighteenth- and nineteenth-century buildings, 24 of which are individually listed in the National Register of Historic Places.

Philadelphia is proud to have been the city in which Thomas Jefferson wrote the Declaration of Independence. Charlottesville takes pride in Jefferson's founding of a university there. Fredericksburg feels honored, for it was from the meeting of the Committee of Revisors there (from January 13 to January 17, 1777) that the statute that would alter the course of the country evolved.

3
EXPERIENCES AT FREDERICKSBURG

I reached Fredericksburg the day after I left you,
and this place on Christmas-day, having felt no more sensation of cold
on the road than if I had been in a warm bed.
—Thomas Jefferson

When Jefferson and his comrades arrived in Fredericksburg in 1777, they were met with a town bristling with military activity. Troops were drilling in the public square and filled the crowded streets, buildings and shops. Awaiting travel orders were the men of the Second Virginia and the Seventh Virginia, ordered here on January 9 for a rendezvous just prior to marching to join General Washington at the front.

By the time Jefferson arrived in Fredericksburg, sixty of the more than four hundred battles and skirmishes of the war had already taken place. On January 12, the very day before Jefferson and the committee began their work, General Hugh Mercer died from bayonet wounds suffered nine days earlier at the Battle of Princeton. Mercer's apothecary shop stood one block away from where the committee met. Today, Mercer's statue rises one hundred yards from the Religious Freedom Monument memorializing Jefferson's bill.

Before they got down to business, Jefferson stopped at the watchmaker to have his timepiece mended and dropped into the local barbershop. There, he saw John Atkinson, the wig maker and barber whose shop was located on the southwest corner of the intersection of George and Caroline Streets, just

Continental Infantry,
by Henry Alexander
Ogden, 1897. *Library
of Congress.*

down from the tavern where they would stay. Jefferson kept a record of these rendezvous as he did with all his travels.

During their stay, Jefferson and the other members of the committee took advantage of this opportunity to spend some relaxing hours with the group at the tavern, who showed them the sights of the town and then offered them the hospitality of the homes of Fredericksburg. Mann Page, a well-known Fredericksburg citizen, made his coach and driver available to visit the sights of the town and to see the local gunnery and weaving mill.

Jefferson's visit in 1777 was not his only social call to the City of Fredericksburg. He often traveled to the city en route to and from his estate, Monticello. Often, he wrote correspondence to his friends and associates there.

To Mann Page:

Philadelphia Dec. 8. 1793.
Dear Sir
I owe you a letter which should have been written by your servant from Fredericksbg. [sic], whom you were so kind as to send for me when I was there. But I had passed the day at Chatham, was returning about dusk,

shivering, and snowing, when I met your servant in the streets. I desired him to apologize to you for my not writing, by telling you the place and state in which he found me, and I left Fredericksbg. [sic] the next morning an hour before day. I shall endeavor to repair all this in person about the 2ᵈ. week in January, when I shall be at Fredericksburg on my way home. I have directed horses to meet me there on the 12ᵗʰ. and whatever time can intervene between my reaching Fredericksbg. [sic] and the 12ᵗʰ. I will certainly have the pleasure of passing with you if you should be at home. I inclose [sic] you a newspaper which contains some interesting things. Our information from France is very chaotic. We can only distinguish that they have gained three important victories on the side of Flanders, and those said to be gained over them are very problematical. Their enemies however still hold Toulon.—I am one of those who believe in the impossibility of the resurrection of monarchy in France and of another campaign by the combined powers. Congress have not yet fully assembled, nor by any vote shewn their complexion. We hope it will be patriotic and republican, but not in the stile [sic] of republicanism of the 1ˢᵗ. and 2ᵈ. Congress. Your brother is not yet arrived. My best respects to Mrs. Page, and am dear Sir with great affection & respect Your friend & servt.
Th: Jefferson

To Hartman Elliot:

Monticello Feb. 15. 1794.
Sir
I received three days ago your favor of January 18. and am sorry to find by it that your driver has defrauded you of ten dollars. I was to pay you for your stage 5. dollars a day for seven days, and ferriages. I paid the ferriages and toll to Fredericksburg myself, exactly 2. dollars, and at Fredericksburg I paid your driver thirty five dollars for the stage, two dollars for his ferriages and toll…and 1. dollar gratuity. This I copy from my travelling memorandums, to which I have recurred. I also took his receipt in the following words. "Received of Thomas Jefferson thirty five dollars for the hire of Mr. Hartman's carriage from Baltimore to Fredericksburg, and two dollars ferriages in full this 12ᵗʰ. day of January 1794. John Williams." And I now inclose [sic] you the original receipt. Besides this my memory serves to assure me there was no mistake in counting the money: for in the morning before my arrival at Fredericksburg I remember counting 30. dollars and placing them in the top of my portmanteau, where I could

get at them easily; and as soon almost as I arrived at Fredericksburg I called him in, paid him the 30. dollars, added a 5. dollar Baltimore bank note which I had received from Mr. Brent and had in my waistcoat pocket, and two other dollars for the ferriages, the amount of which I did not know in the morning as I had still another river to cross. I went in the afternoon into the country, but returned between 9. and 10. the next morning, saw and spoke with your driver, and he had then an opportunity of mentioning any error in counting money, if there had been any. But I know there had been none, and so does he. I am Sir your humble servt [sic]
Th: Jefferson

To Mary Jefferson Eppes:

Philadelphia [June 6, 1798]
My dear Maria.
*I wrote you last on the 18*th. *of May since which* [I have received Mr. Eppes's] *letter of May 20. and yours of May 27. I have deter*[mined to set out from] *this place on the 20*th. *inst. and shall, in my letters of tomorrow,* [order my horses] *to meet me at Fredericksburg on the 24*th. *and may therefore be at home on the 26*th. *or 27*th. *where I shall hope to have the happiness of meeting you. I can supply the information you want as to your harpsichord. your sister writes me it is arrived in perfect safety except the lock & a bit of a moulding broke off. she played on it and pronounces it a very fine one, though without some of the advantages of hers, as the Celestine for instance. if I did not mistake it's* [sic] *tone, it will be found sweeter for a moderate room, but not as good as hers for a large one.*

I forward for mr Eppes some further dispatches from our envoys. to this it is said in addition that mr Pinckney is gone into the South of France for the health of his daughter, Mr. Marshall to Amsterdam, perhaps to come home for orders, and mr Gerry remains at Paris. they have no idea of war between the two countries, and much less that we have authorized the commencement of it.

I will convince you at Monticello whether I jested or was in earnest about your writing. and as, while it will relieve me, it may habituate you to an useful exercise, I shall perhaps be less scrupulous than you might wish. my friendly salutations to mrs Eppes, the two gentlemen & family. to yourself the most tender & constant affection & Adieu
Th: Jefferson

To Thomas Mann Randolph:

Philadelphia June 7. 98.
Th:J. to TMR.
I wrote to my dear Martha on the 31ˢᵗ· of May. hers of the 12ᵗʰ· May is the last I have received from Belmont. I have now determined to leave this on the 20ᵗʰ· inst. [sic]. *I shall be obliged to you therefore to order Jupiter to set out in time to be at Fredericksburg on Sunday the 24th. instant. he must bring my chair, and three horses, because I have a workman to carry with me. this admits him to set out on Saturday morning the 23ᵈ· and consequently allows another post to arrive at Milton with any change of orders should any thing* [sic] *arise the ensuing week to occasion a change, though I have not the least idea any thing* [sic] *will. yet be so good as to call for your letters arriving at Milton Friday the 22ᵈ· in time to give Jupiter his final orders that evening. I send you some further dispatches from our envoys. to the intelligence these contain, I may add I believe on good grounds (tho* [sic] *not quite certain) that Pinckney is gone to the South of France for the health of his family, Marshall to Amsterdam (but whether on his way here for orders or not is not entrusted to us) and Gerry remains at Paris. it is suspected, & indeed believed that a schism has taken place between Gerry & his colleagues. possibly therefore Gerry may make a treaty with the Directory if the brig Sophia does not arrive too soon to let it be completed* [sic]. *it is evident that a relinquishment of claims for spoliations (which the instructions to our envoys authorized* [sic]*) might have been proposed as an equivalent for the loan the French asked as a token of friendship. yet this relinquishment appears never to have been offered by the envoys. it is clear however they did not dream of war between the two countries, much less that it would be commenced by us & bottomed on what they had written. however it is pretty substantially begun by the several bills past; & to put it beyond the possibility of avoidance you will see in the papers resolutions brought in to declare the treaty void, & to authorize general reprisals. the President refused to receive a new Consul general (Dupont) from France, who in consequence departed with Volney & others for France last Monday. Colo. Innes's situation is desperate. we look to every day to be his last. my tenderest affections to my dearest Martha, and to the little ones, and every cordial wish for yourself. Adieu.*
P.S. mr Eppes & Maria set out the 20ᵗʰ· inst. [sic] *from Eppington for Monticello. mrs Trist & mr Trist leave this in a few days for Albemarle.*
Th: Jefferson

To Martha Jefferson Randolph:

Philadelphia Dec. 27. 98.
My dear Martha
I reached Fredericksburg the day after I left you, and this place on Christmas-
day, having (thanks to my pelisse) felt no more sensation of cold on the road
than if I had been in a warm bed. nevertheless I got a small cold which
brought on an inflammation in the eyes, head ach [sic] *&c so that I kept*
within doors yesterday & only took my seat in Senate to-day [sic]. *I have*
as yet had little opportunity of hearing news; I only observe in general that
the republican gentlemen whom I have seen consider the state of the public
mind to be fast advancing in their favor. whether their opponents will push
for war or not is not yet developed. no business is as yet brought into the
Senate, & very little into the other house: so that I was here in good time. I
shall be at a loss how to direct to you hereafter, uncertain as I am whether
you will leave home & where you will be. on this subject you must inform
me. present me affectionately to mr Randolph, and kiss all the little ones
for me, not forgetting Elleanoroon. be assured yourself of my constant and
tender love. Adieu my ever dear Martha.
Th: Jefferson

To Robert Lewis:

Monticello Nov. 10. 24.
Sir
I am very sensible of the kindness of the Common hall and citizens of
Fredericksburg in the invitation which you are so good as to communicate
to partake of a dinner which will be given to Gen La Fayette [sic] *in*
that place. my affection for him and my respect for the Common hall and
citizens of Fredericksburg would render a compliance equally a duty and
gratification. but age & debility put this out of my power. at this moment
too I am additionally disabled by being in a state of convalescence only after
an illness of some continuance which has much weakened me. I pray you
therefore to present my thanks to the Common hall and citizens for this mark
of their attention, to assure them of my high respect and consideration and
to accept yourself a like assurance.
Th: Jefferson

To John Hankart:

Washington June 28. 1803.
Sir
I received yesterday only your favor of the 18th. my whole crop of tobo. [sic]
was put into the hands of my agent at Richmond (being about 45,000.
℔) who in his last letter informed me he was about to sell it at 7½ Dollars
the hundred, and I presume it is actually sold, as I had desired it should be.
were it still on hand I could not withdraw a few hogsheads from it without
greatly injuring the sale of the residue; the purchasers always suspecting
that the best hogsheads have been picked out for the first sale. mr Madison,
the Secretary of state has now at Fredericksburg a very choice crop of
tobacco of the same quality with mine. whether he has engaged it or not I
do not know. Accept my salutations & respect
Th: Jefferson

To William H. Cabell:

Washington July 31. 07.
Dear Sir,
I shall tomorrow set out for Monticello, considering the critical state of things,
it has been thought better, during my stay there, to establish a daily *conveyance*
of a mail from Fredericksburg to Monticello. this enables me to hear both from
the North & South every day. should you have occasion then to communicate
with me, your letters can come to me daily by being put into the Fredericksburg
mail, every day except that on which the mailstage [sic] leaves Richmond for
Milton, by which letters of that day will come to me directly.

The course which things are likely to hold for some time has induced me
to discontinue the establishment at Lynhaven for obtaining daily information
of the movements of the squadron in that neighborhood. but still as it is
expected that a troop of cavalry will patrole [sic] that coast constantly, I
think it would be adviseable [sic] if your Excellency would be so good as
to instruct the commanding officer of the troop, to inform you daily of the
occurrences of the day, sending off his letter in time to get to Norfolk before
the post hour. this letter, after perusal for your own information I would ask
the favor of you to forward by the post of the day under cover to me. I think
a post comes one day from Norfolk by the way of Petersburg, and the next
by the way of Hampton. if so, the letters may come every day. I salute you
with great & sincere esteem & respect.
Th: Jefferson

1791.
Sep. 2. paid for making ruffles 6. D.
pd James market money 5. D. clothes 5.73 D.
  wages for Aug. & Sep. 12 D.
recd from the bank 157 D.
pd Hiltzheimer for pasturing horses 4. D.
pd Ingles his acct. £ 5 – 17 – 3 = 15.63
pd Francis his wages for Aug. 7. D. & board Sep. 8. D.
gave mr Remsen to give to Ducomble when
he discharges him 6. D.
pd Ducomble his wages for Aug. 6. D.
      his disbursements 12/10 ½
pd Jacob his wages for Aug. 6. D. & gave him 6. D.
  on his discharge.
pd Bertault the Upholsterer in full 32 D.
recd from J. Madison balce of what I sent him June 21. July 6. 18.4
paid him in part towards my expences of journey to Virga 8. 4 D.
paid Leslie for an Odometer 10. D.
Diary of journey to Monticello.
set out from Philadelphia

	360 ths a mile	miles	time	
Chestertown.		15	- - - -	lodged. pd J. M. town expences 10. D
3. Wilmington.		13	- - - -	breakft. pd mend Odometer .5
Newport rather hilly, loam or clay	1552	4		
Christeen loam. level.	2060.	6		dined.
Aitkens's	2769.	7¾		
4. Head of Elk hilly. clay.	1755	4¾	- - - -	lodged. brkft. dined. pd J. M. s. D.
North East hilly. gravel or clay	2593	7½	- - -	
Charlestown. gravel or clay gilly. then level.	1100.	3.		
Susquehanne ferry. level & clay then hilly & gravel	2350.	6½	- - -	lodged.
5. Bushtown gravel. very hilly	4232	11¾	- - - -	breakft.
Webster. very hilly. clay or gravel.	4765.	13¼	- - - -	dined & lodged
6. Baltimore excessive hilly. mostly gravel. some clay	4622	12¾	- - -	brkft. qu. if measure. pr pamphlet .2
Elkridge ferry. gravel. rather hilly.	2808	7¾	- - -	dined.
Spurrier's hilly. sand.	2090.	5¾	- - -	lodged
Willet's. hilly. sand.	4500.	12½		

these measured were on the belief that the wheel of the Phaeton made exactly 360 revolutions in a mile, but on measuring it accurately at the end of the journey it's circumference proved such that 354.95 revolutions in a mile made the mile. 1891. or a mile ought to have been greater.

A page from Jefferson's memorandum book. *Massachusetts Historical Society.*

Jefferson maintained meticulous memorandum books that kept track of his ongoing transactions. Below are Jefferson's notes from dealings made in Fredericksburg. Note the notations for January 1777, when Jefferson was in town with the Committee of Revisors.

1768:
Sep 29.   Pd. Mrs. Rathell for 2 pr. shoes 36/.

1769:
April 6. Mem. send Thompson Mason 20 bushels of spring wheat to Fredericksburg to the care of James Mercer.
July 30.   Gave Jupiter to bear expences [sic] *to Fredg. 5/.*

1771:
Mar 19.   Repd. James Maury postage 7½d.

1773:
June 21. Pd. a taylor [sic] *for cutting out clothes for Bob 9d.*

1775:
June 14. Pd. Alexr. Spotswood for a horse (The General) £25. & gave him an order on H. Skipwith for £25. more, the balance. He was got by Janus & is 6. years old.
June 15. Borrowed of Weedon 13/6

1777:
Jan 13.   Pd. barber in Fredsbgh. 1/3.
Jan 14.   Gave M. Page's coachman 1/3.
Jan 15.   Pd. for seeing gunnery 5/.
Pd. for seeing weaving 1/3.
Jan 16.   Pd. for mending watch
Pd. Smith, tavern keeper Fredsbgh., entt. £4–4.
Jan 17.   Pd. Smith's tavern (on the road) entertt. 5/9.

1790:
June 7. Overpd. him also 3/—gave Bob for expences [sic] *to Fredsbg. £8.*

1794:

Jan 12.   pd. Hartman's driver from Baltimore here my share of stage hire 30.D. ferrges. 2.D.

Fredsbg. gratuity 1.D.=33. (delivered him the 5.D. put into my hands by Mr. Brent as his share to Geo. town)

1798:

July 1. Fredsbg. pd. at Benson's keeping horses & my own bill 14.09

vales .75. Long's ordinary.

supper &c. 2.17

vales .25

1807:

Nov 6. D. Brent charity for Fredsbg 100. do.

1819:

Apr 4. Inclosed [sic] *to Wm. F. Gray an order on P. Gibson for 43.25 for bookbinding*

4

WEEDON'S TAVERN

I was honor'd with your Excellency's Letter of Yesterday at this place.
—George Weedon to Thomas Jefferson

T he location that has received credit for lodging Jefferson and his confidants while formulating the Virginia Statute for Religious Freedom is Weedon's Tavern, temporarily known as Smith's at the time of their stay.

Jefferson kept meticulous notes in his memorandum books. His 1777 edition notes his activities:

> *17: Pd. Smith, tavern keeper, Fredsbgh., entt £4-4.*
> *Pd. Smith's tavern (on the road) entertt. 5/9.*

The tavern was originally named for George Weedon, a local proprietor who fought in the French and Indian War and was later named a brigadier general in the Revolutionary War. He married into the tavern business and ran one of the most popular—if not the most popular—inns in the area. It was often a site of ardent debates between the local citizens leading up to the declaration of war against England. According to local historian Paula S. Felder, the tavern occupied lots 25 and 26 in the northwest corner of Caroline and William Street. Others believe the nearby Rising Sun Tavern at 1304 Caroline Street was the location of the historic site.

The tavern was first known as Gordon's Ordinary, a public drinking house that served both locals and passersby. The original owner was John

Weedon's Tavern. *Thomas Jefferson Institute for the Study of Religious Freedom.*

Gordon, who immigrated to Virginia from Scotland in 1721. In 1735, he came to the city and established the inn. He remained its proprietor until his death in 1749. Margaret Gordon, his wife, took over running the inn, renaming it Mrs. Gordon's Tavern. Her daughter Catherine married then Captain George Weedon, who purchased the tavern in its entirety in 1773. The inn flourished under Weedon's ownership, and he became a respected and influential member of the community. Since Weedon was a Mason, the tavern became a center for Masonic activity. Meetings were held on a regular basis, including the organization's annual dinner.

Other highly influential patrons, including George Washington and Thomas Jefferson, made the tavern a regular stop. Many ledgers in Washington's journals during the early 1770s listed dining with political dignitaries at Weedon's Tavern. Playing cards was another favorite pastime at the inn. It is said that as a frequent loser, Washington complained that the Fredericksburg locals were too smart for him. As time went on, the tavern began to regularly serve those outside the town, including those in the adjacent Spotsylvania County.

In addition to fulfilling his role as innkeeper, Weedon expanded his livelihood as a manager of the local Jockey Club. The organization had been established by William Fitzhugh. Fine purebred horses lived in stables that were built behind the inn. Weedon managed the well-being of the horses and arranged for races at the local fair. Sometimes, the animals provided rides for the guests for an additional charge. Beyond lodging, the tavern also served as a local store. In addition to staples such as meat and produce, special items were available.

As a local gathering place, the tavern became a regular meeting ground for citizens to debate politics. This was especially evident in the years leading up to the Revolutionary War. Ironically, many patrons who frequented the tavern were among the most influential men of Virginia. They included Patrick Henry, John Marshall, Hugh Mercer, George Mason, Richard Henry Lee and his brother Harry "Lighthorse" Lee and Gustavus Wallace.

When the war approached, Weedon took a lieutenant colonel's commission in the Third Virginia Regiment. He eventually leased the tavern to William Smith in March 1776 to join the militia full time. Smith planned to continue the inn's service. Weedon was promoted to the rank of full colonel, and the Third Virginia was soon ordered to join the Continental Army in New York City. (He remained with Washington's army and fought in several major battles. The regiment would eventually see action in the New York Campaign, the Battles of Trenton, Princeton, Brandywine, Germantown and Monmouth and the Siege of Charleston.)

When General Benedict Arnold and General William Phillips threatened Virginia in 1781, Weedon organized a battalion of local militia to engage the traitor. On January 12, 1781, Jefferson wrote a letter to Colonel Weedon to let him know that more troops were on the way.

> *Richmond Jany. 12. 1781*
> *Sir*
> *Hearing of 744 Militia from Rockbridge and Augusta and Rockingham on the road through Albemarle, I have sent orders to meet and turn them down to Fredericksburg, where they will expect your orders: They are commanded by Colo. Sampson Mathews. You will* [be pleased] *to observe that as all these were to be rifle Men* [sic] *they were to bring their own field Officers.*
>
> *Baron Steuben has sent Colo. Loyauté the bearer of this to me, and proposed that we should avail ourselves of his Services as an Artillerist for the protection of Fredericksburg. As this matter is entirely in your hands, I beg leave to refer him to you altogether. He is desirous of carrying thither some brass 24. ‡bers from New Castle. They are without Carriages and of course if mounted on batteries would be in extreme danger of being taken. I had moreover ordered them to the forks of James River as a place*

of safety. Nevertheless should they be absolutely necessary for you, you will take them, for which this will be your Warrant.
T.J.

A few weeks later, Jefferson once again wrote to Weedon to apologize for being unable to send supplies.

Richmond Jan. 21. 1781
Sir
I am very sorry we shall not be able to furnish you with a supply of lead until we receive some for which we have sent up the river. The Southern army has been entirely furnished from hence. Five tons were sent to the Northern army last fall. This had reduced our stock very low; and of what was left, one third was destroyed by the enemy. There remains on hand but a small parcel which is now making up at the laboratory. Should however the enemy's movements indicate an intention of visiting you, we will send you what we have, which I think may be done in time to supply the expenditure of what you have. The money press has not yet got to work. As soon as it does I shall be very glad to have money furnished for the purpose of enlisting men, which I consider as a very important one. I suppose it is impossible for you to engage them without the ready money. The bounty is 2000 dollars which should certainly be paid on demand. My last intelligence of the enemy was that their troops were on shore in the Isle of Wight, and their shipping at Newport's news and Hampton road.
I am with great respect Sir your most obedt. servt.,
Th: Jefferson

Ten days later, Jefferson wrote Weedon again, as he was able to procure supplies in Fredericksburg.

Richmond Jan. 31. 1791.
Sir
I am glad that the Commissioners of the provision law in your neighborhood have agreed to lend their aid in furnishing you with provisions. They are certainly justifiable as that law has been reenacted by the assembly. As soon as a force began to collect at Fredericksburg I directed the Commissary Brown (who is authorized by the law to instruct the Commissioners in what is to be expected from them) to take immediate measures for procuring subsistence for those forces either by sending a deputy or applying to the Commissioners.

Your arrangements for the defence [sic] *of Potowmac* [sic] *and Rappahanoc* [sic] *appear to have been judicious. Baron Steuben coming here soon after the receipt of your letter I referred to him to do in that what he should think best, as it is my wish to furnish what force is requisite for our defence* [sic] *as far as I am enabled, but to leave to the commanding officers solely the direction of that force. I make no doubt he has written to you on that subject.*

I am with great respect Sir your most obedt. humble servt.,
Th: Jefferson

After the Continental Army defeated General Cornwallis's forces at Yorktown, a Great Peace Ball was hosted by Weedon at his tavern. On November 11, 1781, American and French officers, politicians, wealthy planters and domestic and foreign dignitaries attended the ball. General George Washington attended, as did the Marquis de Lafayette, who arrived arm and arm with Washington's mother, a local Fredericksburg resident.

During Weedon's absence in 1777, the tavern, called Smith's at the time, played host to Thomas Jefferson's Committee of Revisors as Jefferson drafted the Virginia Statute for Religious Freedom. Weedon missed the entire incident.

After the war ended, Weedon remained the inn's proprietor for a while longer, as his efforts were more focused as a member of the local council and a church vestryman. He retired from innkeeping to become the mayor of Fredericksburg in 1785. He built a stunning home he called Sentry Box in lower Fredericksburg. The house overlooks the Rappahannock River and remains standing.

George Weedon died in 1793, and his wife, Catherine, passed away in 1797. They were both buried in the Masonic Cemetery in Fredericksburg.

On October 19, 1807, tragedy struck. On the corner of Princess Anne and Lewis Streets lay the body of William Standard, whose funeral was set to take place. It is believed that the chimney at the residence sparked a fire that quickly engulfed the building. Standard's body was barely retrieved in time. Adding to the calamity was a strong wind that blew across the dry town and spread the fire rapidly.

Ironically, William Taylor, an agent for Mutual Assurance Society, had his office in a building that is now referred to as the Lewis Store on Caroline Street. In it, he stored many of the records that provided much information on the town. He was at the funeral parlor when the fire originally started and made it out of the house with the roof ablaze.

Hugh Mercer Apothecary Shop, by Francis Benjamin Johnson, circa 1927–1929. *Library of Congress.*

The fire quickly spread to the south and east of the town with no mercy. Surprisingly, the small house on the corner that is now referred to as the Hugh Mercer Apothecary Shop was spared. Three full blocks and sections of two others were completely destroyed. Fortunately, there were no fatalities.

William Taylor recalled, "The thickest and best improved part of the town is now in ashes, very upwards of 200 houses are entirely destroyed, and to add to the calamity of nearly 100 families in distressed situation in consequence thereof....Believe me, this the most awful scene."

The city's ability to fight the fire was limited. The equipment on hand was no match for the raging flames. People began to panic and weren't able to think clearly enough to save their property before the flames reached them. The newspaper wrote that there was "consternation that prevailed destroying concert and presence of mind in most of those who were laboriously active."

Warehouses full of tobacco along the river went up in flames, including the building that was on the site of the Old Stone Warehouse. The Bank-House, located on the site of the current Shiloh Baptist Church (Old Site), also burned to the ground. From there, sparks flew over the river and burned

Top: Weedon's Tavern tabletop marker 1. *Devry Becker Jones, HMdb.org.*

Bottom: Weedon's Tavern tabletop marker 2. *Dawn Bowen, HMdb.org.*

the outhouses and haystacks on the Washingtons' farm (Ferry Farm). The fire completely consumed Weedon's Tavern, known as Benson's at that time.

After the massive destruction and loss of property from the "great fire," the city focused more on firefighting. The town was divided into zones, residents patrolled the streets as lookouts and water cisterns were kept in central locations. Another series of fires broke out in the 1820s before people began constructing outbuildings and stables out of brick. The town would not again see destruction on the scale of the 1807 fire until the Civil War.

Two tabletop markers once stood at the intersection of William and Caroline Streets across from the location of Weedon's Tavern. They have since been removed, as the focus of that corner is now on the civil rights movement, according to the senior historic resources planner. The first said:

Constructed shortly after Fredericksburg's founding in 1728, the tavern across the intersection became a popular gathering place under the proprietorship of its first owner, John Gordon, and then of his son-in-law George Weedon. George Washington was sometimes a guest there.

In January 1777, the Virginia Assembly's Committee of Law Revisors met at the tavern. William Smith rented and operated the establishment, as Colonel Weedon was in New Jersey with General Washington's Continental Army. Weedon's brother-in-law, Hugh Mercer, was also serving with Washington. Mercer, a doctor in civilian life, had practiced in an office just one block to the north. He died of wounds at the battle of Princeton, while the Committee was meeting in Fredericksburg.

The tavern burned in a fire that swept through these blocks in 1807.

On January 9, 1777, Thomas Jefferson arrived at Weedon's Tavern to organize the committee that would recodify the laws of the newly established Commonwealth of Virginia. Painting by Cliff Satterthwaite. Researched and commissioned by Paula S. Felder.

The second said:

Three months after the Continental Congress declared independence from Britain, the Virginia Assembly held its first session, in Williamsburg, on October 7, 1776. The revolutionary government appointed Thomas Jefferson and four other delegates to a Committee of Law Revisors, asking them to rewrite Virginia's Colonial laws to reflect the principles of the new government. Over the next few years, the committee would present 126 statutes to the Assembly for adoption.

In January 1777, the committee began its work at Weedon's Tavern (on the opposite side of this intersection). The tavern owner, George Weedon, had long been an ardent supporter of American independence and was then in New Jersey commanding Virginia troops in George Washington's Continental Army. The American forces included large numbers of African American soldiers. Many of them would receive their freedom after the war, even as slavery expanded in the South.

5
OVERVIEW

In every country and in every age, the priest has been hostile to liberty. He is always in alliance with the despot, abetting his abuses in return for protection to his own.
—Thomas Jefferson

Politically, Jefferson has best been defined as an "enlightened nationalist." As such, he was a proponent of the theory that all areas had to be governed by reason. This, of course, included religion. In a letter to Benjamin Rush, Jefferson stated, "For the use of…reason…every one [*sic*] is responsible to the God who has planted it in his breast, as a light for his guidance, and that, by which alone he will be judged. I have sworn upon the altar of God eternal hostility against every form of tyranny over the mind of man." To support this predictability, a new nation required complete religious freedom and the separation of church and state.

Before the American Revolution, the state of Virginia was home to a single official church, the Church of England. Those citizens of the crown who opposed the church were often discriminated against and prosecuted. Jefferson later referred to these incidents as "the severest contests in which I have ever been engaged."

A year before he wrote the Virginia Statute for Religious Freedom, Jefferson drafted *Resolutions for Disestablishing the Church of England and for Repealing Laws Interfering with Freedom of Worship:*

Jefferson line engraving by
T. Johnson, 1887. *Library
of Congress.*

[Before November 19, 1776]
Resolved &c.

That the statutes 1.E.6.c.1.5 *&* 6.E.6.c.1. 1.El.c.2. 23.El.c.1.
28.El.c.6. 35.El.c.1. 1.Jac.1.c.4. 3.Jac.1.c.1. 3.Jac.1.c.4. 3.Jac.1.c.21.
and the act of ass. 1705.c.6. & so much of all other acts or ordinances
statutes as prescribe punishments for the offence of opinions
deemed heretical *render criminal the maintaining any opinions in
matters of religion or the exercising any mode of worship whatever or as
prescribe punishments for the same;* and all acts or statutes, acts or
ordinances made against, *ought to be repealed.*

Resolved that it is the opn [sic] *of this Commee* [sic] *that so much
of the sd.* [sic] *petitions as prays that the establishment of the Church
of England by law in this Commonwealth may be discontinued, and that
no pre-eminence may be allowed to any one Religious sect over another,
is reasonable; & therefore that the several laws establishing the sd.
Church of England, giving peculiar privileges to* the *it's* [sic] *ministers*
thereof, *& levying for the support thereof* the same *contributions on
the people independent of their good will ought to be repealed; saving to
such incumbents as are now actually seised* [sic] *of Glebe lands, their*

rights to such Glebe lands during their lives, & to such parishes as have received private donations for the use of *support of the sd.* [sic] *Church* of England *the perpetual benefit of such donations.*

These resolutions were undoubtedly drafted prior to November 19, for on that date, the House of Representatives adopted the following:

Resolved…*that all and every act or statute, either of the parliament of* England *or of* Great Britain, *by whatever title known or distinguished, which renders criminal the maintaining any opinions in matters of religion, forbearing to repair to church, or the exercising any mode of worship whatsoever, or which prescribes punishments for the same, ought to be declared henceforth of no validity or force within this Commonwealth.*

Jefferson realized that the only way to ensure that the state's—and later the country's—citizens had the freedom to practice religion as they saw fit was to draft an official proclamation. Without religious freedom, nobles and church officials threatened to create a holy aristocracy. Due to Jefferson's devout theism and firm belief that his relationship with God was a very personal matter, his assertion that "he owes account to none other for his faith or his worship" was the major theoretical foundation to his statute.

According to *The Thomas Jefferson Encyclopedia,* Jefferson's demand for strict separation and religious freedom did not mean that he was irreligious. In fact, this canard irritated Jefferson. He explained:

[T]*he priests indeed have heretofore thought proper to ascribe to me religious, or rather antireligious sentiments, of their own fabric, but such as soothed their resentments against the Act of Virginia for establishing religious freedom. they wished him to be thought Atheist, Deist, or Devil, who could advocate freedom from their religious dictations. but I have ever thought religion a concern purely between our god and our consciences, for which we were accountable to him, and not to the priests.*

The establishment of the Virginia Statute for Religious Freedom was not the only controversy that plagued Jefferson regarding a national stance on religion. Some detractors, then and even now, accuse Jefferson of condoning several government proclamations of a day of prayer. The first was a day of fasting and prayer in response to the British imposition of the Intolerable Acts after the Boston Tea Party. The second occurred when Jefferson was governor and accepted the Continental Congress's request that each governor issue a proclamation for a day of prayer.

Unlike the two previous presidents, President Jefferson expressed hesitancy to endorse proclamations that could be interpreted as religious. He wrote in a letter to Reverend Samuel Miller on January 23, 1808, in response to the reverend's proposal that he recommend a national day of fasting and prayer.

> *I consider the government of the United States as interdicted by the Constitution from intermeddling with religious institutions, their doctrines, discipline, or exercises.…Certainly no power to prescribe any religious exercise, or to assume authority in religious discipline, has been delegated to the general government.…But it is only proposed that I should recommend, not prescribe a day of fasting and prayer. That is, that I should indirectly assume to the United States an authority over religious exercises, which the Constitution has directly precluded them from…civil powers alone have been given to the President of the United States and no authority to direct the religious exercises of his constituents.*

That said, it is interesting to note that Jefferson publicly offered up prayer in both of his inaugural addresses. However, in his mind, there was a clear distinction between an official making a public declaration of faith and an official call to prayer.

Despite his nontraditional view of Christianity, President Jefferson often attended Sunday services in the House of Representatives. When not inhabited by Congress, the House had authorized the usage of the building by different denominations and for some civic functions. In retirement, Jefferson attended church services in the Albemarle Courthouse. Due to Jefferson attending church services in these two government-sanctioned buildings, the suggestion arose that Jefferson did not really support a strict separation of church and state. Jefferson's mindset regarding the use public forums for religious services can be traced to the establishment of the University of Virginia, perhaps Jefferson's most beloved achievement.

Jefferson's original plan for the school was heavily criticized by potential donors, because he did not wish to have a professor of theology or a chapel on site. In response, the board recommended that the university establish "religious schools on the confines of the University…enabling the Students… to attend religious exercises with the Professor of their particular sect." With the threat to the school removed, Jefferson suggested that private religious schools might be established "near" the school grounds but not actually on the university's property.

It's not surprising that Jefferson wanted to keep religion and education at arm's length. Throughout his life, he openly revealed his displeasure for the traditional teaching techniques of Christianity. In a letter to Timothy Pickering on February 27, 1821, Jefferson wrote:

> [N]o one sees with greater pleasure than myself the progress of reason in it's [sic] advances towards rational Christianity. when we shall have done away the incomprehensible jargon of the Trinitarian arithmetic, that three are one, and one is three; when we shall have knocked down the artificial scaffolding, reared to mask from view the simple structure of Jesus, when, in short, we shall have unlearned every thing [sic] which has been taught since his day, and got back to the pure and simple doctrines he inculcated, we shall then be truly and worthily his disciples: and my opinion is that if nothing had ever been added to what flowed purely from his lips, the whole world would at this day have been Christian. I know that the case you cite, of Dr Drake, has been a common one. the religion-builders have so distorted and deformed the doctrines of Jesus, so muffled them in mysticisms, fancies and falsehoods, have caricatured them into forms so monstrous and inconceivable, as to shock reasonable thinkers, to revolt them against the whole, and drive them rashly to pronounce it's [sic] founder an imposter. had there never been a Commentator, there never would have been an infidel. in the present advance of truth, which we both approve, I do not know that you and I may think alike on all points. as the Creator has made no two faces alike, so no two minds, and probably no two creeds. we well know that among Unitarians themselves there are strong shades of difference, as between Doctors Price and Priestley for example. so there may be peculiarities in your creed and in mine. they are honestly formed without doubt. I do not wish to trouble the world with mine, nor to be troubled for them these accounts are to be settled only with him who made us; and to him we leave it, with charity for all others, of whom also he is the only rightful and competent judge. I have little doubt that the whole of our country will soon be rallied to the Unity of the Creator, and, I hope, to the pure doctrines of Jesus also.

Jefferson's attitude toward what he believed to be the improper teaching of Christianity fell on the Protestant clerics and the Roman Catholic Church. This was despite the fact that he counted some Protestant clergymen among his friends. During his time in France just before the French Revolution, Jefferson was deeply suspicious of Catholic priests, considering them a force for reaction and ignorance. In private letters, he indicated that he was wary of too much interference by Catholic clergy in matters of civil government. He wrote in letters: "History, I believe, furnishes no example of a priest-ridden people maintaining a free civil government" and "the priest has been hostile to liberty."

Beyond the clergy, Jefferson always sought a clear distinction that no one, especially the government, had the right to infringe on anyone's faith. In his March 4, 1805 *Drafts of Address of Second Inaugural*, Jefferson stated:

> *In matters of religion, I have considered that its free exercise is placed by the constitution independent of the powers of the general government. I have therefore undertaken, on no occasion, to prescribe the religious exercises suited to it; but have left them, as the constitution found them, under the direction and discipline of state or church authorities acknowledged by the several religious societies.*

Deriving from this statement, Jefferson believed that the government's relationship with the church should be indifferent, religion being neither persecuted nor given any special status. Contrary to popular belief, the term "separation of church and state" does not appear anywhere in the Virginia Statute for Religious Freedom. Jefferson's reply (the following is addressed to Jefferson) to the "Address of the Danbury Baptists Association in the State of Connecticut, Assembled October 7, 1801" was the first time it was used:

> *To Thomas Jefferson, Esq., President of the United States of America.*
> *Sir,*
> *Among the many million in America and Europe who rejoice in your election to office; we embrace the first opportunity which we have enjoyed in our collective capacity, since your inauguration, to express our great satisfaction, in your appointment to the chief magistracy in the United States: And though our mode of expression may be less courtly and pompous than what many others clothe their addresses with, we beg you, sir, to believe that none are more sincere.*
>
> *Our sentiments are uniformly on the side of religious liberty—that religion is at all times and places a matter between God and individuals—that no man ought to suffer in name, person, or effects on account of his religious opinions—that the legitimate power of civil government extends*

no further than to punish the man who works ill to his neighbors; But, sir, our constitution of government is not specific. Our ancient charter together with the law made coincident therewith, were adopted as the basis of our government, at the time of our revolution; and such had been our laws and usages, and such still are; that religion is considered as the first object of legislation; and therefore what religious privileges we enjoy (as a minor part of the state) we enjoy as favors granted, and not as inalienable rights; and these favors we receive at the expense of such degrading acknowledgements as are inconsistent with the rights of freemen. It is not to be wondered at therefore; if those who seek after power and gain under the pretense of government and religion should reproach their fellow men—should reproach their order magistrate, as a enemy of religion, law, and good order, because he will not, dare not, assume the prerogatives of Jehovah and make laws to govern the kingdom of Christ.

Sir, we are sensible that the president of the United States is not the national legislator, and also sensible that the national government cannot destroy the laws of each state; but our hopes are strong that the sentiments of our beloved president, which have had such genial effect already, like the radiant beams of the sun, will shine and prevail through all these states and all the world, till hierarchy and tyranny be destroyed from the earth. Sir, when we reflect on your past services, and see a glow of philanthropy and good will shining forth in a course of more than thirty years we have reason to believe that America's God has raised you up to fill the chair of state out of that goodwill which he bears to the millions which you preside over. May God strengthen you for your arduous task which providence and the voice of the people have called you to sustain and support you enjoy administration against all the predetermined opposition of those who wish to raise to wealth and importance on the poverty and subjection of the people.

And may the Lord preserve you safe from every evil and bring you at last to his heavenly kingdom through Jesus Christ our Glorious Mediator.
Signed in behalf of the association, Nehemiah Dodge
Ephraim Robbins
Stephen S. Nelson

Thomas Jefferson's letter to the Danbury Baptist Association:

To messers. Nehemiah Dodge, Ephraim Robbins, & Stephen S. Nelson, a committee of the Danbury Baptist association in the state of Connecticut.

Jefferson to Danbury, Connecticut, Baptist Association, 1802. *Library of Congress.*

Gentlemen,
The affectionate sentiments of esteem and approbation which you are so good as to express towards me, on behalf of the Danbury Baptist association, give me the highest satisfaction. My duties dictate a faithful and zealous pursuit of the interests of my constituents, & in proportion as they are persuaded of my fidelity to those duties, the discharge of them becomes more and more pleasing

Believing with you that religion is a matter which lies solely between Man & his God, that he owes account to none other for his faith or his worship, that the legitimate powers of government reach actions only, & not opinions, I contemplate with sovereign reverence that act of the whole American people which declared that their legislature should "make no law respecting an establishment of religion, or prohibiting the free exercise thereof," thus building a wall of separation between Church & State. Adhering to this expression of the supreme will of the nation in behalf of the rights of conscience, I shall see with sincere satisfaction the progress of those sentiments which tend to restore to man all his natural rights, convinced he has no natural right in opposition to his social duties.

I reciprocate your kind prayers for the protection & blessing of the common father and creator of man, and tender you for yourselves & your religious association, assurances of my high respect & esteem.

Th: Jefferson

Jan. 1. 1802

6

THE GREAT AWAKENING

Catch on fire, and people will come for miles to see you burn.
—John Wesley

The original thirteen colonies, Virginia, Massachusetts, Maryland, Connecticut, Rhode Island, North Carolina, South Carolina, New York, New Jersey, New Hampshire, Pennsylvania, Delaware and Georgia, were ruled under three different religious institutions. New England's established state church was the Puritans' Congregational Church. The southern colonies were overseen by the Anglican Church, and the middle colonies had a Christian pluralism, though often unharmonious, of various Christian denominations.

In the early years, British colonies attempted to enforce strict religious observance through both colony governments and local town rules. Laws mandated that everyone attend a house of worship and pay taxes to fund the salaries of ministers.

A movement toward a new freedom of religious beliefs grew in the 1700s due to the Bible-based declarations of religious tolerance supporters, such as John Locke and William Penn. This led to a Great Awakening in the 1740s. Though most colonists in the early 1700s lived in colonies with an official state church (the Congregational or Anglican Church), state churches gradually granted more tolerance for other denominations.

The Great Awakening brought various philosophies, ideas and doctrines to the forefront of Christian faith. Some of the major themes included: all

George Whitefield Preaching, by Pieter Elder. *ArtUK*.

people are born sinners; sin without salvation will send a person to hell; all people can be saved if they confess their sins to God, seek forgiveness and accept God's grace; all people can have a direct and emotional connection with God; and religion shouldn't be formal and institutionalized but personal.

This movement greatly affected the religious climate in the colonies and encouraged believers to make a personal connection to their God instead of relying on a church minister. Although new denominations began to establish themselves and immediately boosted church growth, it also caused division among those who did and did not agree with this newfound philosophy.

It had a major effect in reshaping the Congregational Church, the Presbyterian Church, the Dutch Reformed Church and the German Reformed denomination, and it strengthened the small Baptist and Methodist denominations. It had little impact on Anglicans and Quakers.

One evangelist of note, George Whitefield, traveled throughout England and the colonies sharing the Gospel. He was not only a popular preacher but also perhaps the most well-traveled individual in the colonies due to his popularity among the throngs of believers to whom he preached. Many give him credit for the widespread revival that took place during his tours of

Ben Franklin portrait by
Bryan Henry Hall, 1879.
Library of Congress.

BENJAMIN FRANKLIN

America. Often, he would have to preach to crowds in the open air, as the churches were not large enough to handle his audiences.

Due to Whitefield's immense popularity, other minsters became incredibly jealous of him. Some churches would not allow him to use their building, forcing him to preach outside. On several occasions, he spoke to over thirty thousand people. His style was loud and dramatic and instilled a fiery emotion in the crowd. He had a gift that enabled him to spread the Gospel with strength and enthusiasm. As a proponent of religious freedom who recognized no denominational boundaries, Whitefield proclaimed:

> *Father Abraham, who have you in heaven? Any Episcopalians? No! Any Presbyterians? No! Any Independents or Methodist? No, no, no! Whom have you there, then Father Abraham? We don't know those names here! All who are here are Christians—believers in Christ, men who have overcome by the blood of the Lamb and the word of his testimony. Oh, is that the case? Then God help me, God help us all, to forget having names and to become Christians in deed and in truth!*

JOHN ADAMS,

President of the United States of America

John Adams portrait by James Smither, 1797. *Library of Congress.*

During his life, Whitefield made seven tours of the colonies and preached eighteen thousand sermons. Jefferson's fellow founder Benjamin Franklin was particularly fascinated with Whitefield's speaking and the effects he had on people. Though Franklin never openly became a Christian himself, he did become a friend of Whitefield and his official publisher in America. Franklin was impressed with the spiritual impact the preacher's gospel had on society. Franklin wrote that it seemed as if the entire country was growing so religious that one could not walk through the town without hearing psalms sung on every street.

In John Jay's *Notes on Conversations with Benjamin Franklin, 19 July 1783–17 April 1784*, he recalls Franklin's son being baptized by Whitefield:

> *Dr. Franklin lived at Pha. in the Neighbourhood of Mr Boudinot the Father of Elias Boudinot the present Presidt. of Congress—the Father was a Silver Smith [sic] who had come from NYork to settle at Pha., a man much devoted to Whitefield, by whom his Son was baptized Elias after the Prophet of that Name.*

In a letter to Jefferson, Adams cites Whitefield's assertion that there is not a distinction of denomination in the afterlife—a person is not a Quaker, Baptist, Presbyterian, Episcopalian, Catholic or Protestant in heaven. He wrote:

> *Quincy*
> *Dec 3. 13*
> *I know of no Philosopher, or Theologian, or Moralist ancient or modern more profound; more infallible than Whitefield, if the Anecdote that I have heard be true.*
> *He began; "Father Abraham!" with his hands and Eyes gracefully directed to the Heavens as I have more than once Seen him; "Father Abraham," "who have you there with you?" "have you Catholicks?" No. "Have you Protestants." No. "Have you Churchmen." No. "Have you Dissenters." No. "Have you Presbyterians?" No. "Quakers?" No. "Anabaptists?" No. "Who have you then? Are you alone?" No.*
> *"My Brethren! you have the Answer to all these questions in the Words of my Text, He who feareth God and worketh Righteousness, Shall be accepted of him."*

Jefferson echoed the sentiment in a letter to Miles King in which he also cites Whitefield's sermon:

> *Monticello Sep. 26. 14*
> *Sir*
> *I duly recieved* [sic] *your letter of Aug. 20. and I thank you for it, because I believe it was written with kind intentions, and a personal concern for my future happiness. whether the particular revelation which you suppose to have been made to yourself were real or imaginary, your reason alone is the competent judge. for, dispute as long as we will on religious tenets, our reason at last must ultimately decide, as it is the only oracle which god has given us to determine between what really comes from him, & the phantasms of a disordered or deluded imagination. when he means to make a personal revelation he carries conviction of it's* [sic] *authenticity to the reason he has bestowed as the umpire of truth. you believe you have been favored with such a special communication. your reason, not mine, is to judge of this: and if it shall be his pleasure to favor me with a like admonition, I shall obey it with the same fidelity with which I would obey his known will in all cases. hitherto I have been under the guidance of that*

portion of reason which he has thought proper to deal out to me. I have followed it faithfully in all important cases, to such a degree at least as leaves me without uneasiness; and if on minor occasions I have erred from it's [sic] dictates, I have trust in him who made us what we are, and knows it was not his plan to make us always unerring. he has formed us moral agents, not that, in the perfection of his state, he can feel pain or pleasure from any thing we may do: he is far above our power: but that we may promote the happiness of those with whom he has placed us in society, by acting honestly towards all, benevolently to those who fall within our way, respecting sacredly their rights bodily and mental, and cherishing especially their freedom of conscience, as we value our own. I must ever believe that religion substantially good which produces an honest life, and we have been authorised [sic] by one, whom you and I equally respect, to judge of the tree by it's [sic] fruit. our particular principles of religion are a subject of accountability to our god alone. I enquire after no man's, and trouble none with mine: nor is it given to us in this life to know whether your's [sic] or mine, our friend's or our foe's are exactly the right. nay, we have heard it said that there is not a quaker or a baptist, a presbyterian or an episcopalian, a catholic or a protestant in heaven: that, on entering that gate, we leave those badges of schism behind, and find ourselves united in those principles only in which god has united us all. let us not be uneasy then about the different roads we may pursue, as believing them the shortest, to that our last abode: but, following the guidance of a good conscience, let us be happy in the hope that, by these different paths, we shall all meet in the end. and that you and I may there meet and embrace is my earnest prayer: and with this assurance I salute you with brotherly esteem and respect.
Th: Jefferson

Many historians claim that the Great Awakening influenced the Revolutionary War by encouraging the notions of nationalism and individual rights. The Great Awakening was the first time that citizens of the colonies were encouraged to defy principles instituted on them by the Crown. Religion and self-determination were new principles that could work together. That belief was amplified as the eve of the American Revolution dawned, and the followers of the Great Awakening were inspired to fight for the freedom and independence of their country.

The spiritual revolution preceded the actual Revolution. John Adams, in correspondence from 1818, wrote of the events that led up to the Revolution:

The Revolution was effected before the war commenced. The Revolution was in the minds and hearts of the people; a change in their religious sentiments of their duties and obligations. This radical change in the principles, opinions, sentiments and affections of the people was the real American revolution.

The Great Awakening reinvigorated religion in America at a time when it was steadily declining and introduced ideas that would penetrate into American culture. founding fathers such as Thomas Jefferson, James Madison and John Adams viewed this awakening as more than just a stand against religious conformity. The colonies became increasingly tolerant and democratic. Rooted in Bible-based, Judeo-Christian thought, the principles of freedom of belief, religious tolerance and separation of church and civil government would later become more widely accepted and practiced principles in American law.

In 1776, one year before Jefferson authored his statute, the Virginia Declaration of Rights stated:

> *That religion, or the duty which we owe to our Creator and the manner of discharging it, can be directed by reason and conviction, not by force or violence; and therefore, all men are equally entitled to the free exercise of religion, according to the dictates of conscience; and that it is the mutual duty of all to practice Christian forbearance, love, and charity towards each other.*

The declaration was adopted unanimously by the Fifth Virginia Convention at Williamsburg, Virginia, on June 12, 1776, as a separate document from the Constitution of Virginia, which was later adopted on June 29, 1776. Ironically, James Madison proposed liberalizing the article on religious freedom. In 1830, the Declaration of Rights was incorporated within the Virginia State Constitution as article I, but even before that, Virginia's Declaration of Rights stated that it was "the basis and foundation of government" in Virginia.

Religious freedom for all and the separation of church and state would be inspired by the Great Awakening, declared in the Virginia Declaration of Rights and Virginia Statute for Religious Freedom and then implemented, secured and fully realized by the U.S. Constitution and Bill of Rights.

7

THOUGHTS ON RELIGION

Question with boldness even the existence of a god.
—Thomas Jefferson

Jefferson is also a perplexing personality when considering the practice of faith (see appendix D). In a letter written to his associate, John Adams, in January 1817, he boldly states, "Say nothing of my religion. It is known to my god and myself alone."

So, what were Jefferson's personal feelings on spirituality, and why was his Virginia Statute for Religious Freedom one of the three things he deemed worthy enough to inscribe on his grave marker? Certainly, in addition to authoring the Declaration of Independence and founding the University of Virginia, this act remained so near and dear to his heart that he wanted to preserve it for eternity.

Religion remains a hotly debated aspect of Thomas Jefferson's legacy. Some claim that he was simply a Deist, while others have accused him of having no faith at all. Jefferson would have been "officially" categorized as a reformed Protestant and was raised as an Episcopalian (Anglican). However, his tendency for wanting to possess a broader knowledge and understanding of all things led him to be influenced by English Deists who believed in the concept that a higher power did indeed exist but that man's affairs were not under its influence.

Scholars at Monticello conclude that Jefferson was a devout Theist. "Theism is the belief in God, the supreme, self-existent reality who is distinct from and

Jefferson statue, Louisville Metro Hall, Kentucky. *Library of Congress.*

controls the universe. Theism provides a framework for understanding both the material and the spiritual aspects of existence and the natural and moral law. Theism also attributes personal identity and characteristics to God, who is seen as the source and model of human beings."

Jefferson referred to his deity as "our God," "our creator," "Infinite Power which rules the destinies of the universe" and "benevolent governor." In 1823, he denounced atheism in a letter to John Adams, stating, "[T]he God whom you and I acknowledge and adore." His views on the afterlife as a

Jefferson statue, *Religious Freedom* (close-up). *K.G. Hawes.*

younger man were conventional and matched those of other traditional religions. Free will and the act of committing good works were the pathway to Heaven and eternal salvation. This, he believed, was an important incentive for ethical behavior.

When John Adams's beloved wife, Abigail, passed away, Jefferson wrote to his grieving friend, assuring him of her place in the afterlife. He wrote:

> *It is of some comfort to us both that the term is not very distant at which we are to deposit, in the same cerement, our sorrows and suffering bodies, and to ascend in essence to an ecstatic meeting with the friends we have loved & lost and whom we shall still love and never lose again.*

Prayer, on the other hand, was not something that inspired Jefferson. As one who rejected the divinity of Christ and did not believe in any of the miracles that were found in the Bible, Jefferson privately doubted the benefits of prayer. That said, he did pray publicly as part of the obligations of his office. He clearly understood the need to convince the citizens of the country that it was a responsibility of humans to worship God. One prayer of note came in his second inaugural address. He prayed:

> *I ask you to join with me in supplications, that he* [that Being whose hands we are in] *will so enlighten the minds of your servants, guide their councils, and prosper their measures, that whatsoever they do, shall result in your good, and shall secure to you the peace, friendship, and approbation of all nations.*

Jefferson rejected the "divinity" of Jesus, but he believed that Christ was a deeply interesting and profoundly important moral or ethical teacher. He also subscribed to the belief that it was in Christ's moral and ethical teachings that a civilized society should be conducted. Cynical of the miracle accounts in the New Testament, Jefferson was convinced that the authentic words of Jesus had been contaminated.

His theory was that the earliest Christians, eager to make their religion appealing to the pagans, had obscured the words of Jesus with the philosophy of the ancient Greeks and the teachings of Plato. These so-called Platonists had thoroughly muddled Jesus's original message. Firmly believing that reason could be added in place of what he considered to be "supernatural" embellishments, Jefferson worked tirelessly to compose a shortened version of the Gospels titled *The Philosophy of Jesus of Nazareth*. The subtitle stated that the work was "extracted from the account of his life and the doctrines as given by Matthew, Mark, Luke and John."

Jefferson explained his work in a letter to Charles Thomson:

Monticello Jan. 9. 16.
My dear and antient friend
An acquaintance of 52. years, for I think ours dates from 1764. calls for an interchange of notice now & then that we remain in existence, the monuments of another age, and examples of a friendship unaffected by the jarring elements, by which we have been surrounded, of revolutions, of government, of party & of opinion. I am reminded of this duty by the receipt, thro' our friend Dr Patterson, of your Synopsis of the four Evangelists. I had procured it as soon as I saw it advertized [sic], and had become familiar with it's [sic] use. but this copy is the more valued as it comes from your hand. this work bears the stamp of that accuracy which marks every thing [sic] from you, and will be useful to those who, not taking things on trust, recur for themselves to the fountain of pure morals. I too have made a wee little book, from the same materials, which I call the Philosophy of Jesus. it is a paradigma [sic] of his doctrines, made by cutting the texts out of the book, and arranging them on the pages of a blank book, in a certain order of time or subject. a more beautiful or precious morsel of ethics I have never seen. it is a document in proof that I am a real Christian, that is to say, a disciple of the doctrines of Jesus, very different from the Platonists, who call me infidel, and themselves Christians and preachers of the gospel, while they draw all their characteristic dogmas from what it's [sic] Author never said nor saw. they have compounded from

the heathen mysteries a system beyond the comprehension of man, of which the great reformer of the vicious ethics and deism of the Jews, were he to return on earth, would not recognise [sic] one feature. if I had time I would add to my little book the Greek, Latin and French texts, in columns side by side, and I wish I could subjoin a translation of Gassendi's Syntagma of the doctrines of Epicurus, which, notwithstanding the calumnies of the Stoics, and caricatures of Cicero, is the most rational system remaining of the philosophy of the ancients, as frugal of vicious indulgence, and fruitful of virtue as the hyperbolical extravagancies of his rival sects.

On April 21, 1803, Jefferson sent a letter to Dr. Benjamin Rush, who was a fellow founding father and devout Christian, explaining his own interpretation of scripture.

Dear Sir,

In some of the delightful conversations with you in the evenings of 1798–99, and which served as an anodyne to the afflictions of the crisis through which our country was then laboring, the Christian religion was sometimes our topic; and I then promised you that one day or other I would give you my views of it. They are the result of a life of inquiry and reflection, and very different from that anti-Christian system imputed to me by those who know nothing of my opinions. To the corruptions of Christianity I am indeed opposed, but not to the genuine precepts of Jesus himself. I am a Christian, in the only sense in which he wished anyone to be: sincerely attached to his doctrines in preference to all others, ascribing to himself every human excellence, and believing he never claimed any other. At the short interval since these conversations, when I could justifiably abstract my mind from public affairs, the subject has been under my contemplation. But the more I considered it, the more it expanded beyond the measure of either my time or information. In the moment of my late departure from Monticello, I received from Dr. Priestley his little treatise of "Socrates and Jesus Compared." This being a section of the general view I had taken of the field, it became a subject of reflection while on the road and unoccupied otherwise. The result was, to arrange in my mind a syllabus or outline of such an estimate of the comparative merits of Christianity as I wished to see executed by someone of more leisure and information for the task than myself. This I now send you as the only discharge of my promise I can probably ever execute. And in confiding it to you, I know it will not be exposed to the malignant perversions of those who make every word

The Jefferson Bible. Open Culture.

from me a text for new misrepresentations and calumnies. I am moreover averse to the communication of my religious tenets to the public, because it would countenance the presumption of those who have endeavored to draw them before that tribunal, and to seduce public opinion to erect itself into that inquisition over the rights of conscience which the laws have so justly proscribed. It behooves every man who values liberty of conscience for himself, to resist invasions of it in the case of others; or their case may, by change of circumstances, become his own. It behooves him, too, in his own case, to give no example of concession, betraying the common right of independent opinion, by answering questions of faith which the laws have left between God and himself. Accept my affectionate salutations.
Th: Jefferson

In 1820, Jefferson returned to his controversial New Testament research. This time, he completed a much more ambitious work titled *The Life and Morals of Jesus of Nazareth Extracted Textually from the Gospels in Greek, Latin, French and English.* The text of the New Testament appears in four parallel columns in four languages. Jefferson omitted the words he thought were inauthentic and retained those he believed were original. The resulting work is commonly known as the *Jefferson Bible*.

Using a razor and gum, Jefferson committed blasphemy. He cut and pasted his arrangement of selected verses from a 1794 bilingual Latin/Greek Bible using the text of the Plantin Polyglot, a French Geneva Bible and the King James Version. He selected excerpts from the gospels of Matthew, Mark, Luke and John in chronological order and combined the narrative with those of another to create a single chronicle.

No supernatural acts of Christ are included, as Jefferson viewed Jesus as strictly human. He also believed that Jesus himself ascribed to a more deistic belief system. In a letter to Benjamin Rush, Jefferson wrote, "I should proceed to a view of the life, character, and doctrines of Jesus, who sensible of incorrectness of their ideas of the Deity, and of morality, endeavored to bring them to the principles of a pure deism." Jefferson also completely denied the resurrection. The book ends with the words: "Now, in the place where He was crucified, there was a garden; and in the garden a new sepulchre, wherein was never man yet laid. There laid they Jesus. And rolled a great stone to the door of the sepulchre, and departed."

Jefferson described the work in a letter to John Adams, dated October 12, 1813:

> In extracting the pure principles which he taught, we should have to strip off the artificial vestments in which they have been muffled by priests, who have travestied them into various forms, as instruments of riches and power to them.…We must reduce our volume to the simple evangelists, select, even from them, the very words only of Jesus, paring off the Amphibologisms into which they have been led, by forgetting often, or not understanding, what had fallen from him, by giving their own misconceptions as his dicta, and expressing unintelligibly for others what they had not understood themselves. There will be found remaining the most sublime and benevolent code of morals which has ever been offered to man. I have performed this operation for my own use, by cutting verse by verse out of the printed book, and arranging the matter which is evidently his, and which is as easily distinguishable as diamonds in a dunghill. The result is an 8vo of 46 pages of pure and unsophisticated doctrines.

In a letter to Reverend Charles Clay, Jefferson described his results: "Probably you have heard me say I had taken the four Evangelists, had cut out from them every text they had recorded of the moral precepts of Jesus, and arranged them in a certain order; and although they appeared but as fragments, yet fragments of the most sublime edifice of morality which had ever been exhibited to man." Most historians feel that Jefferson composed the book for his own satisfaction, supporting the Christian faith as he saw it. He did not produce it to shock or offend the religious community; he composed it for himself, for his devotion and for his own personal assurance.

After completion of the *Life and Morals*, Jefferson shared it with a number of friends, but he never allowed it to be published during his lifetime. The most complete form Jefferson produced was inherited by his grandson Thomas Jefferson Randolph.

The Christian Bible was not the only religious tome to experience Jefferson's examination. His vast collection of books contained many on religion. The *Virginia Gazette*, a newspaper from Williamsburg, served as a bookseller and sold Jefferson a two-volume set of the Quran in October 1765. It was titled *The Alcoran of Mohammed*. George Sale had translated it from Arabic to English in 1734. In his introduction, Sale wrote that the purpose of the book was to help Protestants understand the Quran so they could argue against it. He wrote:

> *Whatever use an impartial version of the Korân may be of in other respects. It is absolutely necessary to undeceive those who, from the ignorant or unfair translations which have appeared, have entertained too favorable an opinion of the original, and also to enable us effectually to expose the imposture.*

Jefferson was twenty-two years old and had been studying law for three years when he obtained the book. Law professors of that time considered the Quran a book of law. Sale expanded on Jefferson's motives:

> *If the religious and civil Institutions of foreign nations are worth our knowledge, those of Mohammed, the lawgiver of the Arabians, and founder of an empire which in less than a century spread itself over a greater part of the world than the Romans were ever masters of, must needs be so.*

To them, the Quran represented the ruling precepts of the Ottoman Empire, governing over 25 million people. Jefferson, as well as the Western world at that time, thought the Quran was the chief representation of Islamic law. Jefferson is known to have studied the book, but it did not affect his practice of law.

Jefferson carried the same anti-Islamic views of his colleagues. He did, however, have the opinion that the Holy Trinity and the humanness of Jesus were parallel in Islam. His experiences dealing with Islamic piracy in the Mediterranean Sea during his presidency caused him to question Islam's legitimacy as a religion.

In 1786, the United States found that it was having to deal directly with the doctrines of the Muslim religion. The Barbary States of North Africa were using the ports to wage a war of piracy and enslavement against all shipping that passed through the Strait of Gibraltar. Thousands of ships were overtaken, and more than one million Europeans and Americans were sold as enslaved people. Congress offered an agreement called the Treaty of Tripoli, negotiated by Jefferson, which stated roundly that "the government of the United States of America is not, in any sense, founded on the Christian religion, as it has in itself no character of enmity against the laws, religion or tranquility of Musselmen [Muslims]."

Many considered this to be a secular affirmation that attempted to buy off the Muslim pirates by the payment of tribute. Soon after, it was discovered that Ambassador Sidi Haji Abdrahaman, Tripoli's envoy to London, had extorted money and took enslaved people. Jefferson later reported to the secretary of state and to Congress his motive was backed by his religious beliefs:

> *The ambassador answered us that* [the right] *was founded on the Laws of the Prophet, that it was written in their Koran, that all nations who should not have answered their authority were sinners, that it was their right and duty to make war upon them wherever they could be found, and to make slaves of all they could take as prisoners, and that every Mussulman who should be slain in battle was sure to go to Paradise.*

Jefferson's prejudice against Islam was questionable in some ways. He insisted on a constitution wherein "neither pagan nor Mahamedan (Muslim) nor Jew ought to be excluded from the civil rights of the Commonwealth because of his religion." Still, to him and his contemporaries, the idea of a Muslim president or even a Muslim citizen was an abstraction. The first American Muslims who traveled to the country, both free and enslaved, may have numbered in the tens of thousands, but at no time was true equality considered accessible.

That said, Jefferson did mention supporting religious freedom for Muslims in writings. He asserted in his autobiography that his original legislation for religious freedom had been intended "to comprehend, within the mantle of its protection, the Jew and the Gentile, the Christian and Mahometan [Muslim], the Hindoo, and Infidel of every denomination."

Late in his life, Jefferson wrote disparaging terms about the religion and the Quran. Beyond his own interpretations, Jefferson discussed religion fervently in correspondence all his life.

To Peter Carr, he wrote on August 10, 1787:

> *Fix reason firmly in her seat, and call to her tribunal every fact, every opinion. Question with boldness even the existence of a god; because, if there be one, he must more approve the homage of reason, than that of blindfolded fear.*

To Benjamin Rush, he wrote on May 31, 1813:

> *[T]he subject of religion, a subject on which I have ever been most scrupulously reserved. I have considered it as a matter between every man and his maker, in which no other, and far less the public, had a right to intermeddle.*

To Miles King, he wrote on September 26, 1814:

> *I must ever believe that religion substantially good which produces an honest life, and we have been authorised* [sic] *by one, whom you and I equally respect, to judge of the tree by it's* [sic] *fruit. our particular principles of religion are a subject of accountability to our god alone. I enquire after no man's, and trouble none with mine: nor is it given to us in this life to know whether your's* [sic] *or mine, our friend's or our foe's are exactly the right.*

To Charles Thomson, he wrote on January 9, 1816:

> *I too have made a wee little book, from the same materials, which I call the Philosophy of Jesus. it is a paradigma* [sic] *of his doctrines, made by cutting the texts out of the book, and arranging them on the pages of a blank book, in a certain order of time or subject. a more beautiful or precious morsel of ethics I have never seen. it is a document in proof that I am a real Christian, that is to say, a disciple of the doctrines of Jesus, very different from the Platonists, who call me infidel, and themselves Christians and preachers of the gospel, while they draw all*

Jefferson's letter writing device. *Michael Aubrecht.*

their characteristic dogmas from what it's [sic] *Author never said nor saw. they have compounded from the heathen mysteries a system beyond the comprehension of man, of which the great reformer of the vicious ethics and deism of the Jews, were he to return on earth, would not recognise* [sic] *one feature. if I had time I would add to my little book the Greek, Latin and French texts, in columns side by side, and I wish I could subjoin a translation of Gassendi's Syntagma of the doctrines of Epicurus, which, notwithstanding the calumnies of the Stoics, and caricatures of Cicero, is the most rational system remaining of the philosophy of the ancients, as frugal of vicious indulgence, and fruitful of virtue as the hyperbolical extravagancies of his rival sects.*

To Thomas Whittemore, he wrote on June 5, 1822:

Monticello June 5. 22.
I thank you, Sir, for the pamphlets you have been so kind as to send me, and am happy to learn that the doctrine of Jesus, that there is but one God, is

advancing prosperously among our fellow-citizens. had his doctrines, pure as they came from himself, been never sophisticated for unworthy purposes, the whole civilised [sic] world would at this day have formed but a single sect. you ask my opinion on the items of doctrine in your catechism. I have never permitted myself to meditate a specified creed. these formulas have been the bane & ruin of the Christian church, it's [sic] own fatal invention which, thro' so many ages, made of Christendom a slaughter house, and at this day divides it into Casts of inextinguishable hatred to one another. witness the present internecine rage of all other sects against the Unitarian. the religions of antiquity had no particular formulas of creed. those of the modern world none; except those of the religionists calling themselves Christians, and even among these, the Quakers have none. and hence alone the harmony the quiet, the brotherly affections, the exemplary and unschismatising society of the Friends. and I hope the Unitarians will follow their happy example. With these sentiments of the mischiefs of creeds and confessions of faith, I am sure you will excuse my not giving opinions on the items of any particular one; and that you will accept at the same time the assurance of the high respect and consideration which I bear to it's [sic] author.
Th: Jefferson

To John Adams, he wrote on April 11, 1823:

The truth is that the greatest enemies to the doctrines of Jesus are those calling themselves the expositors of them, who have perverted them for the structure of a system of fancy absolutely incomprehensible, and without any foundation in his genuine words. and the day will come when the mystical generation of Jesus, by the supreme being as his father in the womb of a virgin will be classed with the fable of the generation of Minerva in the brain of Jupiter. But we may hope that the dawn of reason and freedom of thought in these United States will do away all this artificial scaffolding, and restore to us the primitive and genuine doctrines of this the most venerated reformer of human errors.

Clearly, religion played a major role in the intellectual life of Jefferson. Whether his views and practices failed to fit into a traditionally organized Judeo-Christian doctrine, his exhaustive examination, dissection and authoring of religious studies proved spirituality mattered to him.

Jefferson was a believer, even if he was nontraditional. He absolutely believed in a higher power and referenced "the Creator." He also believed in the moral teachings of the one referred to as Jesus Christ, regardless of whether he believed he was the messiah. In a letter sent to Harvard professor Benjamin Waterhouse in 1822, Jefferson stated, "The doctrines of Jesus are simple, and tend all to the happiness of man."

In Jefferson's mind, this free will of spiritual expression belonged to everyone, including Christians, Jews, Muslims, Buddhists and those we would refer to in modern times as New Age practitioners. At the same time, atheists and pagans also shared the very same freedom to either reject or pursue their own beliefs.

To sanction or officially recognize a single faith (such as Christianity) would not only have been contrary to the founder's intent, but it would also have marginalized a portion of society. Jefferson's statute was all about inclusiveness. It meant that all believers had the same liberties, regardless of the fact that their belief systems completely opposed each other.

8

AUTHORING OF THE STATUTE

Religion, as well as reason, confirms the soundness of those principles on which our government has been founded and its rights asserted.
—Thomas Jefferson

The Virginia Statute for Religious Freedom was originally referred to as "Bill No. 82: A Bill for Establishing Religious Freedom" (see appendix C). In October 1776, the First General Assembly selected a five-man Committee of Revisors to review the existing laws and redraft them for an independent Virginia. The primary responsibility of rewriting these existing laws was assumed by the three attorneys on the committee: Thomas Jefferson, George Wythe and Edmund Pendleton. George Mason and Thomas Ludwell Lee were also members (see appendix A).

The Bill for the Revision of Virginia Laws initiated the project and was submitted by Jefferson in the Virginia House of Burgesses on October 15, 1776. The purpose of the effort was to reform the entire structure of state law to bring it into conformity with republican principles. It read:

> [October 15, 1776]
> *Whereas on the late change which hath of necessity been introduced into the form of government in this country it is become also necessary to make corresponding changes in the laws heretofore in force, many of which are inapplicable to the powers of government as now organised [sic], others are founded on principles heterogeneous to the republican spirit, others which,*

Jefferson engraving from 1867. *Library of Congress.*

long before such change, had been oppressive to the people, could yet never be repealed while the regal power continued, and others, having taken their origin while our ancestors remained in Britain, are not so well adapted to our present circumstances of time and place, and it is also necessary to introduce certain other laws, which, though proved by the experience of other states to be friendly to liberty and the rights of mankind, we have not heretofore been permitted to adopt; and whereas a work of such magnitude, labour, and difficulty, may not be effected during the short and busy term of a session of assembly:

Be it therefore enacted by the General Assembly of the commonwealth of Virginia, and it is hereby enacted by the authority of the same, That a committee, to consist of five persons, shall be appointed by joint ballot of both houses (three of whom to be a quorum) who shall have full power and authority to revise, alter, amend, repeal, or introduce all or any of the said laws, to form the same into bills, and report them to the next meeting of the general assembly.

And to prevent any delay which may happen in the proceedings of the said committee, by the death or disability of any member thereof, Be it farther enacted, That if either of the said members should die, refuse to act, or be disabled by sickness from proceeding in the said work, it shall be lawful for the remaining members to appoint some other person in his stead and place, which person so appointed is hereby declared a member of the said committee, in like manner as if he had originally been appointed by joint ballot of both houses.

And be it farther enacted, That the said committee shall have power to meet at such times and places as they shall think proper for the purpose of proceeding on the said revisal, to appoint a clerk for their ease and assistance in the work, and to send for any copies of records to the clerk in whose custody they are, which such clerk is hereby directed forthwith to transmit to them.

Provided, That such bills so to be prepared and reported by the committee of revisors shall be of no force or authority until they shall have gone through their several readings in both houses of assembly, and been passed by them in such manner and form as if the same had been originally introduced without the direction of this act.

The original agreement by the Committee of Revisors read:

- *The Common Law not to be medled* [sic] *with, except where Alterations are necessary.*
- *The Statutes to be revised and digested, alterations proper for us to be made; the Diction, where obsolete or redundant, to be reformed; but otherwise to undergo as few Changes as possible.*
- *The Acts of the English Common-wealth to be examined.*
- *The Statutes to be divided into Periods: the Acts of Assembly, made on the same Subject, to be incorporated into them.*
- *The Laws of the other Colonies to be examined, and any good ones to be adopted.*
- *Provisoes* [sic] *&c. which wou'd do only what the Law wou'd do without them, to be omitted.*
- *Bills to be short; not to include Matters of different Natures; not to insert an unnecessary word, nor omit a useful one.*
- *Laws to be made on the Spur of the present Occasion, and all innovating Laws, to be limited in their Duration.*

Jefferson drafted the original bill in 1777. Unfortunately, it was tabled after receiving tremendous opposition from influential members of the Church of England. In 1784, Patrick Henry introduced a resolution to the general assembly for a religious tax assessment, which was supported by members of several denominations. Taxpayers could allocate their money to the denomination of their choice. Proponents of the resolution sought to

James Madison, by John
Vanderlyn, 1816. *White
House Collection/White
House Historical Association.*

support religion in general rather than a particular denomination to remind
citizens to respect ethical principles.

Some of the leading statesmen in Virginia, including Richard Henry Lee,
John Marshall and George Washington, supported Henry's resolution. Most
Anglicans and Presbyterians supported the bill. Yet Baptists, Methodists and
Quakers joined Madison and Jefferson in opposing it. Government, they
thought, could not force belief—no matter how well-intentioned.

Jefferson's close friend and confidant James Madison saw an opportunity
to reintroduce his bill. In the summer of 1785, Madison penned a sensational
petition titled *Memorial and Remonstrance Against Religious Assessments*. In it, he
urged the legislature not to pass the general assessment bill. Madison argued
that religion should be left "to the conviction and conscience of every man."
Religion, he wrote, is a right like other rights and liberties, and if Virginians
did not want to allow the legislature to "sweep away all our fundamental
rights," then they must say that it must leave "this particular right untouched
and sacred." Madison believed that giving the state control over religion
would be the same as allowing it to control all liberties. "Either we must say,"
he added, "that they may control the freedom of the press, may abolish the
Trial by Jury, may swallow up the Executive and Judiciary Powers of the
State; nay that they may despoil us of our very right of suffrage, and erect
themselves into an independent and hereditary Assembly or, we must say, that
they have no authority to enact into the law the Bill under consideration."

Copies of Madison's petition were distributed throughout Virginia and
helped create a storm of widespread protest. It was signed and sent to the
legislature by thousands of residents who opposed the notion of an established
church. Numerous other petitions with over eleven thousand signatures were

also sent to the legislators' desks, and nine out of ten condemned the bill for general assessment. Responding to the public outcry, the legislature, when it reconvened, passed Jefferson's bill on January 16, 1786, by a margin of sixty to twenty-seven.

Unfortunately, Jefferson was not present to witness the legislative process, as he was serving as the U.S. minster to France. Not surprisingly, the bill was hugely supported by religious dissenters who had been held captive by the government-sponsored Anglican Church. This group mainly consisted of Presbyterians and Baptists who had labored to worship on their own. When Jefferson learned of the bill's passage, he had the statute translated to French and Italian and distributed to as many people as possible.

Jean François de Saint-Lambert wrote a letter in French to Jefferson on July 27, 1786. In it, he expressed his pleasure with Jefferson's offering:

> *Eaubonne 27 July* [1786]
> *A little check I made, sir, delayed the pleasure I had in receiving Your Letter and my reply. I believe that Your republic has just rendered one of the greatest services that can be rendered to humanity; it is to the peoples who begin to establish reason; it finds too many established prejudices dear The ancient peoples, it is only the Tems, The progress of the lights, and the example that can gradually bring back The reign of This unfortunate reason; Your republics instruct us, sir, and perhaps your institutions will one day do for us what the English philosophers and ours have only led us to hope.*
>
> *It would be very useful if the act of Your assembly were printed in Europe In all languages, it would be to the public papers to spread it, but it must not be entrusted to ours, they would truncate it, they would alter it, or not print it. The courier of Europe and the Leide gazette, that of the two bridges could render this service.*
>
> *Two things especially pleased me in this act, (1) The word of* Religious Freedom *instead of the word of* Tolerance *which I infinitely dislike, because to have the right to* Tolerer *one must have the right to* prevent. *(2) It is to exempt all citizens from giving money to the minister chosen by others. This monk is excellent for forever preventing the clergy from being a formidable body and body, he will have little head and little money.*
>
> *Mde. D'houdetot is very sensitive to Your memory, received my thanks and the assurance of the veneration that You inspired me.*

Madison was especially pleased with the accomplishment. He said the statute was, "a true standard of Religious liberty: its principle the great barrier agst. usurpations on the rights of conscience. As long as it is respected & no longer, these will be safe." In a letter to Madison, Jefferson expressed his pleasure with the reception:

> *Paris Dec. 16. 1786.*
> *Dear Sir…*
> *The Virginia act for religious freedom has been received with infinite approbation in Europe and propagated with enthusiasm. I do not mean by the governments, but by the individuals which compose them. It has been translated into French and Italian, has been sent to most of the courts of Europe, and has been the best evidence of the falshood* [sic] *of those reports which stated us to be in anarchy. It is inserted in the new Encyclopedie* [sic]*, and is appearing in most of the publications respecting America. In fact it is comfortable to see the standard of reason at length erected, after so many ages during which the human mind has been held in vassalage by kings, priests and nobles; and it is honorable for us to have produced the first legislature who has had the courage to declare that the reason of man may be trusted with the formation of his own opinions. I shall be glad when the revisal shall be got thro'….*
> *Th: Jefferson*

In a study titled "The Statute of Virginia for Religious Freedom: A Statute to Liberate the Mind," Richard A. Rutyna writes:

> *In the final analysis, the "Bill for Establishing Religious Freedom" which was enacted by the Virginia General Assembly in 1786 bore the distinct imprint of Thomas Jefferson and James Madison and was, as much as anything else, a testimonial to their commitment to intellectual freedom. The distinguished Pulitzer Prize winning historian, Ryus Isaac, does not exaggerate when he says of the statute that it was a "Manifesto of the freedom of the mind."*

In addition to directly influencing the First Amendment to the U.S. Constitution, the bill also established the United States Supreme Court's understanding of religious freedom.

As posted on Monticello.org: the original manuscript in Jefferson's hand no longer exists. The text of the act as drafted by Jefferson (and approved by the revisors), as well as the changes adopted by the general assembly, is provided in the following section, with the general assembly's insertions shown within brackets:

Well aware that the opinions and belief of men depend not on their own will, but follow involuntarily the evidence proposed to their minds; that [Whereas] *Almighty God hath created the mind free, and manifested his supreme will that free it shall remain by making it altogether insusceptible of restraint; that all attempts to influence it by temporal punishments, or burthens, or by civil incapacitations, tend only to beget habits of hypocrisy and meanness, and are a departure from the plan of the holy author of our religion, who being lord both of body and mind, yet chose not to propagate it by coercions on either, as was in his Almighty power to do, but to extend it by its influence on reason alone; that the impious presumption of legislators and rulers, civil as well as ecclesiastical, who, being themselves but fallible and uninspired men, have assumed dominion over the faith of others, setting up their own opinions and modes of thinking as the only true and infallible, and as such endeavoring to impose them on others, hath established and maintained false religions over the greatest part of the world and through all time: That to compel a man to furnish contributions of money for the propagation of opinions which he disbelieves and abhors, is sinful and tyrannical; that even the forcing him to support this or that teacher of his own religious persuasion, is depriving him of the comfortable liberty of giving his contributions to the particular pastor whose morals he would make his pattern, and whose powers he feels most persuasive to righteousness; and is withdrawing from the ministry those temporal[ry] rewards, which proceeding from an approbation of their personal conduct, are an additional incitement to earnest and unremitting labours for the instruction of mankind; that our civil rights have no dependance on our religious opinions, any more than on our opinions in physics or geometry; that therefore the proscribing any citizen as unworthy the public confidence by laying upon him an incapacity of being called to offices of trust and emolument, unless he profess or renounce this or that religious opinion, is depriving him injuriously of those privileges and advantages to which, in common with his fellow citizens, he has a natural right; that it tends also* [only] *to corrupt the principles of that very religion it is meant to encourage, by bribing, with a monopoly of worldly honours and emoluments, those who will externally profess and conform to it; that though indeed these are criminal who do not withstand such temptation, yet neither are those innocent who lay the bait in their way; that the opinions of men are not the object of civil government, nor under its jurisdiction; that to suffer the civil magistrate to intrude his powers into the field of opinion and to restrain the profession or propagation of principles on supposition of their ill tendency is a dangerous fallacy, which at once destroys all religious liberty, because he being of course judge of that tendency will make his opinions the rule of judgment, and approve or condemn the sentiments of others only as they shall square with or differ from his own; that it is time enough for the rightful purposes of civil government for its officers to interfere when principles break out into overt acts against peace and good order; and finally, that truth is great and will prevail if left to herself; that she is the proper and sufficient antagonist to error, and has nothing to fear from the conflict unless by human interposition disarmed of her natural weapons, free argument and debate; errors ceasing to be dangerous when it is permitted freely to contradict them.*

We the General Assembly of Virginia do enact [Be it enacted by the General Assembly] *that no man shall be compelled to frequent or support any religious worship, place, or ministry whatsoever, nor shall be enforced, restrained, molested, or burthened in his body or goods, nor shall otherwise suffer, on account of his religious opinions or belief; but that all men shall be free to profess, and by argument to maintain, their opinions in matters of religion, and that the same shall in no wise diminish, enlarge, or affect their civil capacities.*

And though we well know that this Assembly, elected by the people for the ordinary purposes of legislation only, have no power to restrain the acts of succeeding Assemblies, constituted with powers equal to our own, and that therefore to declare this act [to be] *irrevocable would be of no effect in law; yet we are free to declare, and do declare, that the rights hereby asserted are of the natural rights of mankind, and that if any act shall be hereafter passed to repeal the present or to narrow its operation, such act will be an infringement of natural right.*

According to the Free Speech Center, the first section, the preamble, affirms "that Almighty God hath created the mind free" and that "to compel a man to furnish contributions of money for the propagation of opinions which he disbelieves and abhors is sinful and tyrannical."

The second section discusses the act itself, stating that "no man shall be compelled to frequent or support any religious worship, place or ministry… or otherwise suffer on account of his religious opinions or belief."

And the third section concludes by offering a warning to future assemblies, declaring that repeal of the act would violate "the natural rights of mankind."

Not everyone accepted Jefferson's proposed statute eagerly. The main arguments against it were that it would lead to moral decay and that it would undermine the authority of the church. Others argued that this separation of church and state went both ways—that religious groups should not interfere with governance. Advocacy groups even argued that politicians should not allow their religious beliefs to influence policy, legislation or court decisions.

Jefferson defended the act's policy and later recounted the birth of the act in his autobiography:

> *Early therefore in the session of 76 to which I returned, I moved and presented a bill for the revision of the laws; which was passed on the 24th of October, and on the 5th of November Mr. Pendleton, Mr. Wythe, George Mason, Thomas L. Lee and myself were appointed a committee to execute the work. We agreed to meet at Fredericksburg to settle the plan of operation and to distribute the work. We met there accordingly on the 13th of January 1777. The first question was whether we should propose to abolish the whole existing system of laws, and prepare a new and complete Institute, or preserve the general system, and only modify it to the present state of things.... This last was the opinion of Mr. Wythe, Mr. Mason & myself. When we proceeded to the distribution of the work, Mr. Mason excused himself as, being no lawyer, he felt himself unqualified for the work, and he resigned soon after. Mr. Lee excused himself on the same ground, and died indeed in a short time. The other two gentlemen therefore and myself divided the work among us....*
>
> *The bill for establishing religious freedom, the principles of which had, to a certain degree, been enacted before, I had drawn in all the latitude of reason & right. It still met with opposition; but with some mutilations in the preamble, it was finally passed; and a singular proposition proved that it's [sic] protection of opinion was meant to be universal. Where the preamble declares that coercion is a departure from the plan of the holy author of our religion, an amendment was proposed, by inserting the word "Jesus Christ," so that it should read "a departure from the plan of Jesus Christ, the holy author of our religion" the insertion was rejected by a great majority, in proof that they meant to comprehend, within the mantle of it's [sic] protection, the Jew and the Gentile, the Christian and Mahometan, the Hindoo, and infidel of every denomination.*

The complexity of Jefferson and his statute did not end there. During Jefferson's term as the governor of Virginia, the Continental Congress sent a circular to the state executives recommending a day of public thanksgiving. Jefferson sent the circular to the Virginia House of Delegates, which wrote out the actual proclamation and sent it for his signature. He signed this proclamation for a day of "Thanksgiving and Prayer," to be held on December 9, 1779. This was interpreted by some to be a religious declaration sanctioned by the state:

Whereas the Honourable the General Congress, impressed with a grateful sense of the goodness of Almighty God, in blessing the greater part of this extensive continent with plentiful harvests, crowning our arms with repeated successes, conducting us hitherto safely through the perils with which we have been encompassed and manifesting in multiplied instances his divine care of these infant states, hath thought proper by their act of the 20th day of October last, to recommend to the several states that Thursday the 9th of December next be appointed a day of publick [sic] and solemn thanksgiving and prayer, which act is in these words, to wit.

Whereas it becomes us humbly to approach the throne of Almighty God, with gratitude and praise, for the wonders which his goodness has wrought in conducting our forefathers to this western world; for his protection to them and to their posterity, amidst difficulties and dangers; for raising us their children from deep distress, to be numbered among the nations of the earth; and for arming the hands of just and mighty Princes in our deliverance; and especially for that he hath been pleased to grant us the enjoyment of health and so to order the revolving seasons, that the earth hath produced her increase in abundance, blessing the labours of the husbandman, and spreading plenty through the land; that he hath prospered our arms and those of our ally, been a shield to our troops in the hour of danger, pointed their swords to victory, and led them in triumph over the bulwarks of the foe; that he hath gone with those who went out into the wilderness against the savage tribes; that he hath stayed the hand of the spoiler, and turned back his meditated destruction; that he hath prospered our commerce, and given success to those who sought the enemy on the face of the deep; and above all, that he hath diffused the glorious light of the gospel, whereby, through the merits of our gracious Redeemer, we may become the heirs of his eternal glory. Therefore,

Resolved, that it be recommended to the several states to appoint THURSDAY the 9th of December next, to be a day of publick [sic] and solemn THANKSGIVING to Almighty God, for his mercies, and of PRAYER, for the continuance of his favour and protection to these United States; to beseech him that he would be graciously pleased to influence our publick [sic] Councils, and bless them with wisdom from on high, with unanimity, firmness and success; that he would go forth with our hosts and crown our arms with victory; that he would grant to his church, the plentiful effusions of divine grace, and pour out his holy spirit on all Ministers of the gospel; that he would bless and prosper the means of education, and spread the light of christian knowledge through the remotest corners of the earth; that he would smile upon the labours of his people, and cause the earth to bring forth her fruits in abundance, that we may with gratitude and gladness enjoy them; that he would take into his holy protection, our illustrious ally, give him victory over his enemies, and render him finally great, as the father of his people, and the protector of the rights of mankind; that he would graciously be pleased to turn the hearts of our enemies, and to dispence [sic] the blessings of peace to contending nations.

That he would in mercy look down upon us, pardon all our sins, and receive us into his favour; and finally, that he would establish the independance [sic] of these United States upon the basis of religion and virtue, and support and protect them in the enjoyment of peace, liberty and safety.

I do therefore by authority from the General Assembly issue this my proclamation, hereby appointing Thursday the 9th day of December next, a day of publick [sic] and solemn thanksgiving and prayer to Almighty God, earnestly recommending to all the good people of this commonwealth, to set apart the said day for those purposes, and to the several Ministers of religion to meet their respective societies thereon, to assist them in their prayers, edify them with their discourses, and generally to perform the sacred duties of their function, proper for the occasion.

Given under my hand and the seal of the commonwealth, at Williamsburg, this 11th day of November, in the year of our Lord, 1779, and in the fourth of the commonwealth.

THOMAS JEFFERSON

In 1786, Jefferson, then a minister of France, sent a letter to his fellow committee member George Wythe, informing him of how well their statute was received overseas:

Paris Aug. 13. 1786.
Dear Sir
The European papers have announced that the assembly of Virginia were occupied on the revisal of their Code of laws. This, with some other similar intelligence, has contributed much to convince the people of Europe, that what the English papers are constantly publishing of our anarchy, is false; as they are sensible that such a work is that of a people only who are in perfect tranquillity [sic]. Our act for freedom of religion is extremely applauded.

The Ambassadors and ministers of the several nations of Europe resident at this court have asked of me copies of it to send to their sovereigns, and it is inserted at full length in several books now in the press; among others, in the new Encyclopedie [sic]. I think it will produce considerable good even in these countries where ignorance, superstition, poverty and oppression of body and mind in every form, are so firmly settled on the mass of the people, that their redemption from them can never be hoped. If the almighty had begotten a thousand sons, instead of one, they would not have sufficed for this task. If all the sovereigns of Europe were to set themselves to work to emancipate the minds of their subjects from their present ignorance and prejudices, and that as zealously as they now endeavor the contrary, a thousand years would not place them on that high ground on which our common people are now setting out. Ours could not have been so fairly put into the hands of their own common sense, had they not been separated from their parent stock and been kept from contamination, either from them, or the other people of the old world, by the intervention of so wide an ocean. To know the worth of this, one must see the want of it here. I think by far the most important bill in our whole code is that for the diffusion of knowledge among the people. No other sure foundation can be devised for the preservation of freedom, and happiness.

Christianity was not the only religion that benefited from religious freedom. The Jewish population also reaped the benefit of worshipping as they pleased. Jefferson wrote to Jacob De La Motta expressing his thanks for receiving a copy of the address given at the opening of a new synagogue.

Monticello
Sep. 1. 20.
Th: Jefferson returns his thanks to Doctr [sic] de la Motta for the eloquent discourse on the Consecration of the Synagogue of Savannah which he has been so kind as to send him. it excites in him the gratifying reflection that his own country has been the first to prove to the world two truths, the most salutary to human society, that man can govern himself, and that religious freedom is the most effectual anodyne against religious dissension: the maxim of civil government being reversed in that of religion, where it's [sic] true form is "divided we stand, united we fall." he is happy in the restoration, of the Jews particularly, to their social rights, & hopes they will be seen taking their seats on the benches of science, as preparatory to their doing the same at the board of government. he salutes Dr de la Motta with sentiments of great respect.

9

INFLUENCE OF FIRST AMENDMENT

The people, not the government, possess the absolute sovereignty.
—James Madison

Freedom of religion was not originally drafted in the U.S. Constitution to Jefferson's liking. In a letter sent from Paris to his friend and fellow founder James Madison on December 20, 1787, two months after the document was signed, Jefferson wrote: "I will now add what I do not like. First the omission of a bill of rights providing clearly & without the aid of sophisms for freedom of religion."

Freedom of religion was adopted on December 15, 1791, as the first of ten amendments that constitute the Bill of Rights. These amendments prevent the government from making laws that regulate an establishment of religion or that prohibit the free exercise of religion. (The Fourteenth Amendment to the U.S. Constitution guarantees the religious civil rights.)

Jefferson did not consider his concept of religious freedom to be a civil agreement between citizens and the government. He believed it to be a natural right of the people. His statute ends with the bold statement: "We are free to declare, and do declare, that the rights hereby asserted are the natural rights of mankind."

The influence of Jefferson's concept of religious freedom can be seen in article VI, section III, of the Constitution known as the Separation Clause:

But no religious test shall ever be required as a qualification to any office or public trust under the United States.

Religious freedom often ignites protests. *Change Comes Slow*.

And the First Amendment to the Constitution, adopted in 1791, provides:

> *Congress shall make no law respecting an establishment of religion, or prohibiting the free exercise thereof.* [The first sixteen words are often referred to as the Religious Liberty Clauses.]

The First Amendment to the U.S. Constitution was directly influenced by the Virginia Statute for Religious Freedom. It prevents the government from making laws that regulate an establishment of religion or that prohibit the free exercise of religion, or abridge the freedom of speech, the freedom of the press, the freedom of assembly or the right to petition the government for redress of grievances.

The amendment commands government to have no interest in theology or ritual; it admonishes government to be interested in allowing religious freedom to flourish—whether the result is to produce Catholics, Jews or Protestants; or to turn the people toward the path of Buddha; or to end in a predominantly Muslim nation; or to produce in the long run atheists or agnostics. On matters of this kind, government must be neutral. This freedom plainly includes freedom from religion, with the right to believe, speak, write, publish and advocate antireligious programs. Its prohibition on an establishment of religion includes many things, from prayer in widely varying government settings over financial aid for religious individuals and institutions to comment on religious questions.

The amendment also makes clear that it sought to protect "the free exercise" of religion or what might be called "free exercise equality." Free exercise is the liberty of persons to reach, hold, practice and change beliefs freely according to the dictates of conscience. The Free Exercise Clause prohibits governmental interference with religious belief and, within limits, religious practice. "Freedom of religion means freedom to hold an opinion or belief, but not to take action in violation of social duties or subversive to good order."

It should be noted that nowhere in this amendment or in the Constitution is the phrase "separation of church and state" mentioned. Jefferson first mentioned the phrase in 1802. He said the First Amendment was written to be a wall of separation between the church and state. The government could not mandate anything about religion and people were free to do as they choose regarding religious beliefs.

James Madison proposed twenty constitutional amendments, and his proposed draft of the First Amendment read as follows:

> *The civil rights of none shall be abridged on account of religious belief or worship, nor shall any national religion be established, nor shall the full and equal rights of conscience be in any manner, or on any pretext, infringed. The people shall not be deprived or abridged of their right to speak, to write, or to publish their sentiments; and the freedom of the press, as one of the great bulwarks of liberty, shall be inviolable. The people shall not be restrained from peaceably assembling and consulting for their common good; nor from applying to the Legislature by petitions, or remonstrances, for redress of their grievances.*

The acknowledgement of religious freedom as the first right protected in the Bill of Rights points toward the American founders' understanding of the importance of religion. Freedom of religion is protected by the First Amendment through its Establishment Clause and Free Exercise Clause, which together form the religious liberty clauses of the First Amendment.

The precise meaning of the Establishment Clause can be traced back to the very beginning. Jefferson wrote about the First Amendment and its

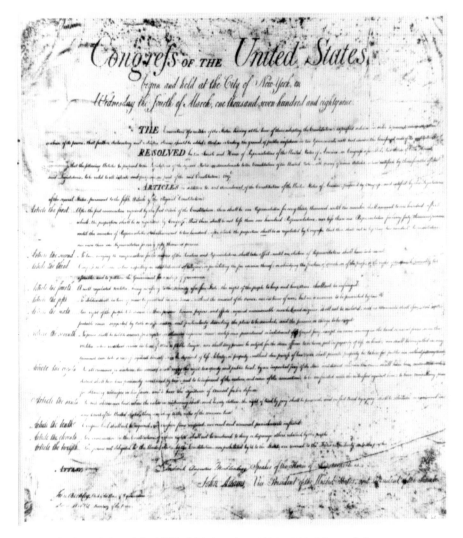

A reproduction of the original Bill of Rights, circa 1920–1930. *Library of Congress.*

restriction on Congress in an 1802 reply to the Danbury Baptists, a religious minority that was worried about the dominant position of the Congregational Church in Connecticut. He wrote:

> *Believing with you that religion is a matter which lies solely between Man & his God, that he owes account to none other for his faith or his worship, that the legitimate powers of government reach actions only, and not opinions, I contemplate with sovereign reverence that act of the whole*

American people which declared that their legislature should "make no law respecting an establishment of religion, or prohibiting the free exercise thereof," thus building a wall of separation between Church & State. Adhering to this expression of the supreme will of the nation on behalf of the rights of conscience, I shall see with sincere satisfaction the progress of those sentiments which tend to restore to man all his natural rights, convinced he has no natural right in opposition to his social duties.

As president, rejecting the precedent of both George Washington and John Adams, Jefferson refused repeated requests that he issue a proclamation for prayer or thanksgiving, insisting that such an official proclamation was outside the powers of the president and inconsistent with the First Amendment.

The ever-evolving relationship between religion and politics can still be seen. To commemorate the bicentennial of the call for a Bill of Rights, the Williamsburg Charter Foundation drafted the Williamsburg Charter in 1988 as a reaffirmation of the principles of religious liberty found in the Bill of Rights. The charter was signed by a wide range of representatives from government and law, education and business, as well as by representatives of the Christian, Jewish, Muslim and Buddhist communities. As described by the First Liberty Institute at George Mason University, it states:

The Charter sets forth a renewed national compact, in the sense of a solemn mutual agreement between parties, on how we view the place of religion in American life and how we should contend with each other's deepest differences in the public sphere. It is a call to a vision of public life that will allow conflict to lead to consensus, religious commitment to reinforce political civility. In this way, diversity is not a point of weakness but a source of strength.

The Williamsburg Charter affirms that America's distinctive stance on religious liberty is not simply a historical landmark, but it is an ongoing challenge to be met in each generation. Today, as the religious landscape of America becomes multireligious, the legacies of Jefferson and Madison are being appropriated anew by denominations of all kinds.

In 1994, Delegate William Howell of Stafford gave what could be considered to be controversial remarks on the state of the First Amendment at the city's annual ceremony commemorating Religious Freedom Day:

Thomas Jefferson's intellect and ability are unsurpassed in the history of the nation. Of his many accomplishments, the three he considered the most significant and that are written on his tombstone were the authorship of the Declaration of Independence and the Statute for Religious Freedom and the creation of the University of Virginia. The Statute for Religious Freedom is indeed a remarkable legacy.

However, a manifestation of that legacy with which Jefferson would probably not concur is that which has been created, compounded and perpetrated by the U.S. Supreme Court since 1947 when deciding cases based upon the establishment clause of the First Amendment to the Constitution.

A little history of the First Amendment will illustrate my position.

One of the principle [sic] authors of the First Amendment was James Madison, who worked closely with Jefferson in the battle in the Virginia legislature for the enactment of the Statute for Religious Freedom. Undoubtedly, Madison's close work with Jefferson provided much of the groundwork for the language in the First Amendment. Jefferson was, of course, in France at the time the Bill of Rights was written and so his input into the drafting of that document was limited.

We are certain, however, of what Madison and the other framers intended from the fairly detailed notes taken during the discussion and debate. And what is perfectly clear is that the framers of the First Amendment were concerned only about the creation of a national church and perhaps to prevent discrimination among the sects.

Nothing in any of the writings of those present would indicate a requirement of neutrality on the part of government with respect to religion.

How is Jefferson implicated in all of this? After all, he was out of the country when the Bill of Rights was written.

In 1802 President Jefferson wrote a letter to the Baptist Association of Danbury, Conn., in response to their inquiry expressing concern that another denomination was to be made the state church.

President Jefferson, in his response, stated that he contemplated "that act of the whole American people which declared that their legislatures should 'make no law respecting an establishment of religion or prohibiting the free exercise thereof' thus building a wall of separation between church and state." Jefferson was clearly referring to the creation of a state religion and not saying that the government must be neutral on religion.

There were, in fact, many examples, before, during and after Jefferson's presidency that illustrate this.

For example, Congress time and again appropriated money for the education of Indians. Typical was Jefferson's treaty with the Kaskaskia Indians which provided funding for the tribe's Roman Catholic priest and church.

And public funding of religion was not limited to Indian tribes. In 1833 Congress authorized Ohio to sell land and use the proceeds for the "support of religion…and for no other purpose whatsoever."

It would seem clear from this evidence that the First Amendment establishment clause had acquired a well-accepted meaning—forbidding the establishment of a national religion and forbidding preference among religious sects and denominations.

The First Amendment did not require neutrality of religion, nor did it prohibit the federal government from providing nondiscriminatory aid to religion. This concept was the law of the land for more than 150 years.

In 1947, however, Justice Hugo Black—writing for the U.S. Supreme Court in the landmark case of Everson v. Board of Education*— stated that "in the words of Jefferson, the clause against the establishment of religion by law was intended to erect a 'wall of separation between church and state."*

Bounding from that faulty premise, the court over the past 47 years has slowly and steadily removed the government from having anything to do with religion. Their interpretation of the First Amendment and the so-called wall of separation has resulted in the removal of any type of prayer or religious observance from public school or many facets of public life. Lower courts have expanded the boundaries even further with such extreme propositions as the unconstitutionality of Bibles in libraries or the banning of crosses on grave markers in public cemeteries or the removal of a poster of the ten Commandments from the hallway of a public school.

As Chief Justice William Rehnquist so aptly stated in the case of Wallace v. Jaffree, *"the wall of separation of church and state is a metaphor based on bad history, a metaphor which has proved useless as a guide to judging. It should be frankly and explicitly abandoned."*

Thomas Jefferson felt to the core of his soul that the rights of the individual were paramount.

To interpret his phrase on the separation of church and state as the building block for these extreme Supreme Court decisions is not only historically fraudulent but a tremendous disservice to the genius we come to remember today.

One can only hope, and, yes, dare I say pray, that the court will someday soon come to its senses and reverse many of these ridiculous decisions.

Predictably, the statute has maintained authority in numerous court cases. This can be traced back to the 1879 case *Reynolds v. the United States*. The United States Supreme Court rejected a claim that Mormon polygamy was protected by the First Amendment, quoting the Virginia Statute to define religious freedom. Over a century later, in 1947, the court likewise declared in *Emerson v. Board of Education* that the religion clauses of the First Amendment to the U.S. Constitution "had the same objective and were intended to provide the same protection against governmental intrusion on religious liberty as the Virginia statute." This interpretation has been broadly accepted in the Supreme Court's legal philosophy, although it has come under attack on occasion by traditional members of the Supreme Court.

10

THOMAS JEFFERSON INSTITUTE

The Institute will serve its purpose best if it has the support of all citizens.
—Thomas Jefferson Institute for the Study of Religious Freedom

The Thomas Jefferson Institute for the Study of Religious Freedom was founded in the City of Fredericksburg to preserve and promote the history of Jefferson's experiences in Fredericksburg in 1777 and the statute that came to be as a result. According to the institutes pledge brochure:

> *The Institute, though not a tourist attraction in the ordinary sense, should become nevertheless a focal point of interest to visitors from all over the United States and abroad by virtue of its uniqueness as a center devoted to a great ideal, that of religious freedom, for which millions have died in the past in all parts of the world. The birthplace of such an ideal as universal tolerance is worthy of a pilgrimage as much as is a battlefield, a historic home or beautiful garden, all of which Fredericksburg can boast of in abundance. Sometimes called "America's Most Historic City," it resounds with the names of George Washington, Mary Washington, James Monroe, John Paul Jones, Fielding Lewis, Matthew Fontaine Maury, R.E. Lee, Clara Barton and many others.*

Article II of the organization's charter states that the purpose of the institute was scientific, educational and cultural study. Its work pertained to the study and advocacy of religious freedom in order to make the concept of freedom in connection with religion meaningful to those living under the U.S. Constitution and its First Amendment as well as others "to whom the right to life, liberty and the pursuit of happiness is accorded."

The institute dedicated itself to performing an important educative function but did not engage in formal teaching. Its overarching goal was to inspire citizens of all ages with respect and appreciation for the Jeffersonian concept of religious freedom. It went further, claiming to be a "moral leaven or catalyst" while implanting the desire for responsible thinking, regard for the beliefs and opinions of others and tolerance and understanding for one's fellow man.

Jefferson chromolithograph, New York, 1893. *Library of Congress.*

By making learning resources and educational activities available to the citizens of Fredericksburg and beyond, the institute provided a respected community service without duplicating the educational facilities that were already established within the city. The plan was to have an immediate impact on the City of Fredericksburg and the surrounding Spotsylvania, Stafford, Caroline and King George Counties.

Membership in the institute was fair: $1.00 for elementary to high school students, $1.50 for college students, $7.50 for a class, $10.00 for an individual, $15.00 for a family, $25.00 for sustaining, $25.00 for church and civic groups, $100 for sponsorships, $500 for patronage and $1,000 for corporations.

Students in private and public schools in all grades that were studying history, religion, social sciences and politics were invited to use the institute's materials and facilities. Teachers wishing to refresh their memories and college students writing research papers were also included. Speakers in search of preparation material on local, state, national or international developments in the field of religious tolerance, civil rights legislation and other problems related to the freedom movement and history would gain great benefit from the institute's collection.

Not just focusing on Fredericksburg, the Institute's scope extended beyond the city's borders and those of the commonwealth to include countries of the world. Freedom of worship was a problem that citizens around the world were facing. The anticipated audience that would be attracted to the institute's offerings were students and scholars from colleges and universities from both near and far.

Dr. Kurt Leidecker, a scholar of comparative religion and chairman of the institute, presented his own worldwide vision for the institute in a letter to the editor in the *Free Lance-Star*:

> *The Thomas Jefferson Institute for the Study of Religious Freedom was established by a committee of the Fredericksburg Bicentennial Commission to commemorate a highly significant event in the annals of the United States. The Institute does not prejudge, condemn, accuse or engage in litigation. It fosters understanding of the world-wide problem of religious freedom and thus makes a positive contribution to church and state relationship and the ecumenical problems on the whole. By upholding, therefore, the kind of religious and intellectual freedom envisaged by Thomas Jefferson, George Mason, James Madison and several other men of the Revolution, Virginia can rightfully be proud.*

He added the impact Jefferson's statute had on the country and beyond:

> *I always say it was a beacon light for people in Europe. In those days they all took their religion seriously—so seriously they would go to war over it. When they came to this country they were relieved of this darkness the religious dogma. The whole attitude in America has contributed tremendously to religious peace in the world.*

Throughout the years in a series or as occasional demands, the institute sponsored lectures, seminars, slide showings, movies, excursions, dinners, receptions and dramatic skits. Talks by cultural representatives of different countries illustrated the progress of religious freedom and toleration in their countries. A symposium was planned in which scholars expounded America's interest in the religions and provided the opportunity for new dimensions in dialogue. Popular talks to audiences of varying sizes were held at a number of venues.

Perhaps the most publicly notable contribution of the institute was the establishment of Religious Freedom Day. Each year, the city marks the anniversary of the meeting of Thomas Jefferson and other Virginians in Fredericksburg and Jefferson's drafting of the Virginia Statute for Religious

Knights of Columbus color guard. *From the* Free Lance-Star.

Shell's presidential coin game
commemorating religious freedom. *Numista.*

Freedom. It starts with a downtown freedom parade and ceremony at the Religious Freedom Monument. Participants represent everyone from Christians and Muslims to humanists and atheists.

In January 1977, the institute hosted a birthday party to celebrate Jefferson's accomplishment, complete with a special message from President Ford and an address from Governor Mills E. Godwin.

In 1985, the institute sold "freedom medals" to commemorate the two hundredth anniversary of the Virginia Statute for Religious Freedom. The bronze medals were designed locally and sold for twenty dollars. Designed by Scott Howson, they were cast by Wegner Metal Arts, where a twenty-five-step process was required to create them. About three inches in diameter, one side depicted the likeness of Jefferson, while the other depicted the dates he drafted the statute in Fredericksburg.

Dr. Leidecker said that they had originally petitioned Congress to issue the medal in 1977, which was the actual two hundredth anniversary of the drafting of the statute. Unfortunately, they denied the request. Leidecker remained dedicated to the project, and all those years later, he finally saw his efforts come to fruition. "We celebrate people," he said in an interview with the *Free Lance-Star.* "Why not celebrate their ideas?"

In addition to creating the official commemoration day and freedom medals, the institute organized a series of events, including a banquet, a community religious freedom service, a public forum, a concert and a play titled *In Search of Religious Freedom.*

Adults were not the only ones who were touched by Jefferson's efforts. A contest between local students in fourth and seventh grades was also sponsored by the institute. The students were prompted to write an essay on the Virginia Statute for Religious Freedom. In their essays, some students referred to events in history.

Michelle Bare, a seventh grader, wrote, "One thing I think about when I say religious freedom is Hitler and the Jews. They were persecuted for something I have the right to do."

Melissa A. Smith referred to John F. Kennedy in her essay: "This was the first time Americans had been asked to accept a Catholic for president and many questioned it and worried over it. He was elected in spite of this and proved that his Catholicism in no way hampered his ability."

Gemma Gonzales said she would have been "one of those who would fight for their religious freedom," although she believed that prayer should not be allowed in public schools because that goes against the separation of church and state.

David Huber spoke of his ancestors: "When immigrants from all over the world began coming to the new world they brought with them new religions and ideas. My great-great-grandfather came over from Germany. He was a Catholic. My great-great-grandmother was a Baptist. They both kept their own religions."

Several years after the institution's founding, Dr. Leidecker was presented with an award for establishing the institute, which flourished under his leadership. He was praised in the *Free Lance-Star*:

To the Editor,

We would like to express deep appreciation to our City Council for the beautifully written and framed Resolution 83-13 which was recently presented to Dr. Kurt F. Leidecker, one of our most distinguished citizens. The resolution expressed gratitude to Dr. Leidecker for establishing in our beloved Fredericksburg, the Thomas Jefferson Institute for the Study of Religious Freedom, Inc. Membership in this institute, which has become worldwide, continues to grow.

Butler Robinson Franklin
Fall Hill

In its declaration, the institute summed up its mission by making the following statement: "The Institute will serve its purpose best if it has the support of all citizens who feel that the ideal for which it was established is not only a good and valid one, but needs constant re-affirmation and application in daily life by every member of the human race."

11

MONUMENT AND MEMORIALS

The United States is an experiment started by Thomas Jefferson
here in Fredericksburg.
—Father Donald J. Rooney

In a town full of historical markers, it's no surprise that the city erected a monument to commemorate Jefferson's presence when he penned the statute. The Fredericksburg City Council elected to commission a stonemason named St. Clair Brooks to create the monument. Brooks set about to create a monument that would complement the space while not dominating the surrounding landscape. According to the city's Policy on New Monuments and Interpretive Signage, "The size and scale of the monument or interpretive sign should fit well with the surrounding context. Emphasis in the City of Fredericksburg is placed on monuments and interpretative signs that do not distract from the historic view and ambience of the location." The result of Brooks's design was a simple, four-sided column. As a testament to its meaning, stones from churches across the country were acquired to form the memorial. Today, there is an eighty-acre park in nearby Falmouth called St. Clair Brooks Park.

The simple yet engaging marker was unveiled on October 16, 1932. Representatives from sixteen of the leading denominations in the United States participated in the commemoration. The monument is the third-oldest memorial referring to the religious statute Jefferson drafted; the two older memorials are his original tombstone at the University of Missouri

Knights of Columbus at the Religious Freedom Monument. *From the* Free Lance-Star.

and his replacement tombstone at Monticello. Jefferson personally selected this contribution to be included on his headstone. A quick search online reveals that there are at least ten other monuments to Jefferson. All feature a likeness of Jefferson on top. Therefore, the design of the Thomas Jefferson Religious Freedom Monument adds to its uniqueness.

Virginia governor John Garland Pollard made these remarks at the dedication ceremony:

> *We are here to do honor to a great man and to rededicate ourselves to a great principle. Our immortal Virginia Declaration of Rights of 1776 reminds us that frequent recurrence to fundamental principles is the price of liberty. In the same declaration we are told "that religion or duty we owe to our Creator, and the manner of discharging it can be directed only by reason and conviction, not by force or violence, and therefore all men are equally entitled to the free exercise of religion according to the dictates of conscience."*
>
> *Nine years after this famous declaration came Jefferson's Statute for Religious Freedom, which placed all religions on a basis of absolute equality before the law.*
>
> *It announced to the world that our civil rights have no dependence on our religious opinions any more than our opinions in physics or geometry,*

and that all men shall be free to maintain their opinions in matters of religion and that the same shall in no ways diminish, enlarge or affect their civil capacities.

This was America's greatest and most distinctive gift to the science of government. Acts of toleration had before been passed, but never before had any government put all religions on a footing of perfect equality.

To the minds of some, religious liberty means the Christian denomination only and to other religions simply toleration. But the word toleration has no place in our political vocabulary, for it carries the implication that we, by our grace, may extend to others the privilege of worshipping God as they may please, while as a matter of fact men do not worship God according to the dictates of conscience by virtue of any man-given right. The gift is direct from God. It is born with us.

Nor is the liberty of which we speak confined to religionists, for man not only has the right to worship God in his own way, but he has an equal legal right not to worship him at all, for as Jefferson said: "Why punish him in this life because we suppose he will be miserable in the life to come?"

Nor can it be said in any true legal sense that this is a Christian nation, for Christians are entitled to no special rights or privileges.

By way of parenthesis, may I say if a politician has any right to an opinion in the realm of the spiritual that there is no such thing as a Christian state even in a religious sense, for—according to my theology—religion is strictly a personal matter. Men are saved not by our states, nor by races, nor by groups, nor by families, but as individuals. Salvation is not a wholesale transaction. It is strictly retail, one by one.

The state has no religious function and, may I add, the church has no political function. I do not consider what I have said inconsistent with my firm belief that the church is by far the greatest single factor in the success of the state, but history proves that both church and state flourish most when they are separate and distinct.

The reason they do not mix is that law rests on force, while religion rests on love. And here, before this distinguished gathering of church leaders, I want to make my acknowledgment as a representative of the state, the debt of gratitude which the state owes you for your yeomen part in creating and maintaining that sentiment of righteousness, without which all laws are important.

Barring some petty pilfering of the rights of minority sects still found in the laws of some of the states, it may be said that religious freedom is firmly established by constitutional and statutory provisions throughout the nation.

What a blessed heritage! We have received without money and without price what our forefathers paid for in rivers of blood.

As we meet here in grateful remembrance of this precious gift so freely handed down to us from the past, may I plead for an enlarged gift to be handed down to our children.

There was a religious tyranny in law, now happily passed away, but there still remains today in all its cruelty, a tyranny which proscribes, ostracizes, denounces and condemns men who dare think for themselves.

The spirit of religious liberty will never be completely enthroned in human hearts until men have a more decent regard for the opinions of others.

I need hardly remind you that in many American communities membership in some religious sects constitutes a social, political and business handicap. Conversely, membership in other sects is considered an asset. Wherever public sentiment allows such conditions to prevail, the spirit of religious liberty is dead.

I can exercise my rights of property and my rights of person in any American community without the slightest criticism, but there are many places where I cannot exercise my freedom of conscience without being made to suffer. And so I plead for a broader and more tolerant spirit toward adherents of other faiths to the end that we may bring to its complete fruition the work which our forefathers so nobly began.

Rights of person, rights of property, rights of conscience. The greatest of these are the rights of conscience. And so as I began. I welcome you to this, our rededication to a noble ideal.

The monument was originally installed on George Street, but in 1977, it was moved to its present location on Washington Avenue. This area is a historical district within the city. It is located on the original grounds of Kenmore Plantation, just steps from the mansion on a small, beautiful, secluded parkway that also holds the Mary Washington and General Hugh Mercer Monuments. The Washington Avenue Historic District is Fredericksburg's only historic monumental avenue and the site of high-style residences built for the city's elite at the turn of the twentieth century. The new location was more fitting for the monument, as it was now among other noteworthy tributes. A brick base and shrubbery were added to complement the structure.

The stone column bears two bronze plaques on each side:

RELIGIOUS LIBERTY

*FROM A MEETING IN FREDERICKSBURG,
JANUARY 13–17, 1777,
OF A COMMITTEE OF REVISORS
APPOINTED BY THE GENERAL ASSEMBLY
OF VIRGINIA, COMPOSED OF THOMAS
JEFFERSON, GEORGE MASON, EDMUND
PENDLETON, GEORGE WYTHE, AND THOMAS
LUDWELL LEE TO "SETTLE THE PLAN OF
OPERATION AND TO DISTRIBUTE THE
WORK"—EVOLVED*

*THE STATUTE OF RELIGIOUS FREEDOM
AUTHORED BY
THOMAS JEFFERSON.*

*IN THIS DOCUMENT
THE UNITED STATES OF AMERICA
MADE PROBABLY ITS GREATEST
CONTRIBUTION TO
GOVERNMENT RECOGNITION OF
RELIGIOUS FREEDOM.*

The opposite side says:

*THIS MEMORIAL
MARKS THE SITE OF A CELEBRATION,
ON OCTOBER 16,1932,
BY REPRESENTATIVES OF THE
LEADING RELIGIOUS FAITHS IN
AMERICA, COMMEMORATIVE OF THE
RELIGIOUS CHARACTER OF
GEORGE WASHINGTON,
WHOSE BOYHOOD HOME TOWN WAS
FREDERICKSBURG;
AND OF THE SEPARATION OF CHURCH
AND STATE, AS THE VIRGINIA
"BILL FOR ESTABLISHING*

RELIGIOUS FREEDOM"
WAS OUTLINED BY A COMMITTEE
CONSISTING OF
THOMAS JEFFERSON, GEORGE MASON,
EDMUND PENDLETON, GEORGE WYTHE
AND THOMAS LUDWELL LEE
WHICH MET IN THIS CITY ON
JANUARY 13, 1777
***
ERECTED BY THE STATE COMMISSION ON CONSERVATION
AND DEVELOPMENT
1932

There are two smaller memorial plaques that were subsequently installed on the ground at each side of the base:

PLACED HERE BY THE RAPPAHANNOCK ASSEMBLY,
KNIGHTS OF COLUMBUS,
IN HONOR OF
RELIGIOUS FREEDOM AND THE 225ᵀᴴ ANNIVERSARY
OF THE DRAFTING BY THOMAS JEFFERSON
OF THE STATUTE OF RELIGIOUS FREEDOM FOR
VIRGINIA
JANUARY 13, 2002

The Knights of Columbus is a global Catholic fraternal service. Founder father Michael J. McGivney wanted to provide a Catholic alternative to secret societies, such as Freemasonry. The four degrees of the Knights of Columbus are based on four principles: charity, unity, fraternity and patriotism.

The opposite plaque says.

IN MEMORY AND APPRECIATION
OF
DR. KURT F. LEIDECKER
(1902–1991)
FOUNDER AND DIRECTOR
OF
THE THOMAS JEFFERSON INSTITUTE

FOR THE
STUDY OF RELIGIOUS FREEDOM
AND
BY WHOSE EFFORTS
THIS MONUMENT WAS RELOCATED TO THIS SITE

Dr. Leidecker of Mary Washington College was instrumental in convincing the city council to move the monument to its current location in the 1970s. Dr. Leidecker was a professor at Mary Washington College from 1948 until his retirement in 1973, and he was a specialist in Buddhism. He was devoted to the promotion of tolerance and cross-cultural understanding. The Mary Washington College Board of Visitors established the Leidecker Center for Asian Studies in 1998.

In 1976, a proposal was made to move the monument from its original location from the Maury School grounds to the north end of Washington Avenue at Pitt Street. The city council's Public Works Committee deadlocked in two-to-two vote. Committee chairman Ferris M. Bellman was displeased with the proposed location and suggested a downtown location. Council members Kathryn H. Massey and Samuel H. Ryan agreed with the plea of Dr. Leidecker, who was acting as the head of the Bicentennial Commission, which was aligned with the Thomas Jefferson Institute for the Study of Religious Freedom.

The theory put forth was to place the monument in a more conspicuous tourist spot. The suggested location was near Kenmore, also known as Kenmore Plantation, a major tourist attraction in the city that was built in the 1770s and was the home of Fielding and Betty Washington Lewis.

Leidecker stated there were two reasons the move would be beneficial beyond its more noticeable location. It would give them the opportunity to capitalize on two bills recently proposed by Representative J. Kenneth Robinson to Congress. First, moving the monument now during the bicentennial would bring national attention to the town. This could result in a special medallion to be cast and placed on the monument. Second, it would set January 17, 1977, as a National Commemoration Day for the two hundredth anniversary of the drafting of the statute.

In addition, the Virginia Landmarks Commission reported that if the monument was to be moved at that time, the cost of $3,200 to do so could possibly be entirely reimbursed. A contractor would be hired to disassemble and move the monument, and a local garden club would provide the landscaping at no cost. The movement of the monument was completed in early 1977.

Kenmore, home of George Washington's sister Betty Washington Lewis. *Library of Congress.*

Every January, at the site of this monument, the City of Fredericksburg pays homage to Jefferson and his foresight to give each Virginian religious freedom. The event attracts representatives from all faiths who appreciate the opportunity to be included in a ceremony recognizing everyone. Each group carries a banner during the parade. Some of them include messages like "Don't Believe in God? You're Not Alone" and "We Are Muslims and

Americans" and the scripture of 1 John 2:2: "And He is the propitiation for our sins." Representatives from the Knights of Columbus form a color guard and carry flags at the front of the procession. Sometimes, members on motorcycles escort them. The parade starts at the downtown train station and ends at the monument. A wreath-laying ceremony follows. In addition, the Fredericksburg mayor's office makes an official proclamation commemorating the bill. An invocation and benediction are also part of the ceremony.

Each year, a keynote speaker addresses the crowd at the end of the journey. In 2014, Speaker William J. Murray, chairman of the Religious Freedom Coalition, expressed his feelings online following the ceremony. He said, "Our freedom in this nation is a gift from God and the core of that freedom is religious liberty. As religious liberty fades, so does every freedom we enjoy. Without religious freedom there is not freedom of speech, as can be seen in other nations. If a government can restrain us from speaking of our faith it can restrain us in any regard. We must do more than cherish our freedoms; we must defend them or lose them, and first among those liberties is religious freedom."

In 2020, the speaker was Father Donald J. Rooney, pastor of Saint Bernadette Church in Springfield, Virginia. His words were exceptionally thought-provoking. He said, "The United States is an experiment started by Thomas Jefferson here in Fredericksburg." He added, "What does religion look like when it is unbound by political power? It is here that we can live lives of a truly spiritual context, free of war lords and prelates who would have political reasons to twist the truths of faith and use them for evil. Here is the place where all are free to be who they are spiritually."

A walking tour to the Thomas Jefferson Religious Freedom Monument is available at the city's visitor center. Each year, thousands of the town's annual 1.5 million tourists include the monument on their list of stops when exploring. The site has been described online as serene, striking and thought-provoking. One five-star review on Tripadvisor referred to it as "Jefferson's brilliance on display."

The Religious Freedom Monument serves a purpose beyond being a mere memorial. Educational groups periodically stop at the monument, using the spirit of the site as a backdrop for dialog. Nearby, Mary Washington University hosts lectures with Jefferson scholars on the subject of Jefferson's statute. The university archives include a manuscript collection from Dr. Leidecker, as well as a collection of papers from former President William M. Anderson on the Jefferson Institute's involvement with Religious

Freedom Day. Local historical and heritage groups maintain the history of the memorial so that it can be preserved. The modest pedestal is one of the city's most cherished monuments.

With Jefferson's interest in architecture and sculpture, including his Greek-inspired estate and obelisk gravestone, one wonders what he would think of the simple square podium standing at attention in the middle of a road. Perhaps he would not appreciate a permanent fixture. In a letter to Margaret Bayard Smith, he wrote, "Architecture is my delight, and putting up and pulling down, one of my favorite amusements." He may not have valued the sentiment at all. Jefferson also wrote, "Could the dead feel any interest in monuments or remembrances of them?"

12

ANNUAL RELIGIOUS FREEDOM DAY

Jefferson himself valued his Fredericksburg project among the three most important
accomplishments of his incredibly productive career.
—Honorary Judge John A. Jamison

First established by the Thomas Jefferson Institute for the Study of Religious Freedom during the 1976 U.S. bicentennial and later assumed by the Knights of Columbus Rappahannock Assembly 1613, the city has come together to commemorate the bill and Jefferson's role in preserving religious freedom in a ceremony for all faiths at the Religious Freedom Monument on Washington Avenue. The event is attended by more than one hundred participants. The appropriate ceremony includes a parade, the laying of a wreath, an invocation, a benediction and a keynote speech.

Often, the parade is led by the Knights of Columbus, followed by groups such as members of the Church of Jesus Christ of Latter-day Saints, the Lutheran Church and members of the local Masonic lodge. Members of all faiths are invited to carry a banner identifying their affiliation and showing support for religious freedom.

The event symbolizes the healthy dialogue and relationships that exist between the city's different religious groups. Each year, the mayor of Fredericksburg issues an official proclamation recognizing the statute:

Proclamation

Whereas, It was in the Town of Fredericksburg, in the month of January 1777, that Thomas Jefferson first presented his Statute for Religious Freedom to a committee of revisors of the Laws of Virginia to make them conform in letter and spirit to the Declaration of Independence: and

Whereas, the Statute was passed January 16, 1786, by the Virginia General Assembly and in March 1789 became the basis for the First Amendment to the Constitution of the United States of America: and

Whereas, still in force, the Statute as the most liberal in the world, guarantees to every citizen freedom of belief and expression, and has since inspired millions of people everywhere: and

Whereas, recognizing the importance of this document in view of the current secular and religious discussions, and carrying out the desire of its author that what he had done for the people be duly remembered.

Now, therefore, I, Lawrence A. Davies, Mayor of the City of Fredericksburg, Virginia, do hereby proclaim this day as Religious Freedom Day.

In addition, a guest speaker is selected to give an address at the base of the Religious Freedom Monument. One of the noteworthy addresses was presented by the Honorary Judge John A. Jamison. In it, he presents an excellent recollection of the events that took place in the city during Jefferson's stay:

Address by Honorary Judge John A. Jamison
Religious Freedom Day, January 13, 1982
Fredericksburg, Virginia

The weather today is indeed appropriate for the occasion. For, on January 13, 1777, as cold as it was, there was an air of excitement in Fredericksburg.

It is overlooked by many historians that our city was a highly important staging area and source of arms, supplies and material for the battle fronts of the Revolution. Factories here were operating full blast and the riverfront was full of ships and sailors.

For my material for this brief talk, I am deeply indebted to Mr. Francis Wilshin, well-known historian who has generously allowed me use of his manuscript for what I believe will be a truly monumental and scholarly history of the early days of Fredericksburg, and I will quote passages from it.

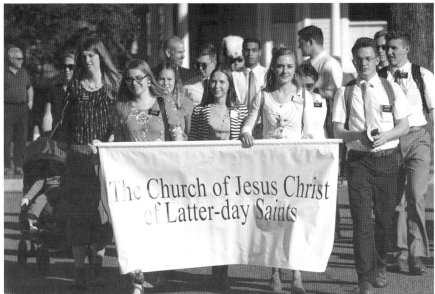

Top: Parade participants representing an atheist organization. *From the* Free Lance-Star.

Bottom: Parade participants representing Mormons. *From the* Free Lance-Star.

PROCLAMATION
RELIGIOUS FREEDOM DAY
January 10, 2021

WHEREAS, it was the town of Fredericksburg, in the month of January 1777, that Thomas Jefferson first presented his Statute for Religious Freedom to a committee of revisors of the laws of Virginia to make those laws conform in letter and spirit to the Declaration of Independence; and

WHEREAS, the Statute was passed January 16, 1786, by the Virginia General Assembly and in March 1789 became the basis for the First Amendment to the Constitution of the United States of America; and

WHEREAS, still in force, the Statute, as the most liberal in the world, guarantees to every citizen freedom of belief and expression, and has since inspired millions of people everywhere; and

WHEREAS, recognizing the importance of this document in view of current secular and religious discussions, and carrying out the desire of its author that what he had done for the people be duly remembered.

NOW, THEREFORE, I, Mary Katherine Greenlaw, Mayor of the City of Fredericksburg, Virginia, do hereby proclaim **January 10, 2021** as

Religious Freedom Day

Mary Katherine Greenlaw, Mayor
City of Fredericksburg, Virginia

Fredericksburg Proclamation. *City of Fredericksburg.*

On that chilly day, by stage and horseback, there gathered at Smith's (later known as Weedon's Tavern in Fredericksburg) a distinguished group of well-known statesmen with a high mission. Weedon's Tavern stood where the Woolworth building now is. Busily intent on their varied activities, only a few townspeople noticed the arrival of these patriots and certainly none envisioned the full scope and dramatic impact on history of their assignment that week. As they drove into town, the members of the group must have been impressed with the martial air of the place—there were heard the sound of the flute, the beat of the drum and the bark of command as soldiers drilled on the public square and crowded the streets, the buildings and the shops. Awaiting travel orders were the men of the Second Virginia and the Seventh Virginia, ordered here on January 9th for a rendezvous just prior to marching to join General Washington at the front.

Meeting as a Committee of Code Revisors, appointed by General Assembly November 1776 were: Thomas Jefferson, author of the Declaration of Independence, George Mason, author of the Virginia Bill of Rights, Edmund Pendleton, President of the Virginia Convention, George Wythe, eminent jurist and legal educator, and Thomas Ludwell Lee, a leading member of the Virginia Assembly. "Their task was awesome—'to settle the plan of operation and to distribute the work,' in a revision of the Virginia Code of Laws so as to conform as to the letter and spirit of the Declaration of Independence."

In those days travel and communication were primitive and the individual colonies which became states, of necessity exercised far more sovereignty and independence than is permitted of the states these days. Virginia, being the leader among the colonies, earned and was keeping that position by having as citizens some of the most brilliant statesmen and legal specialists ever known to the world of law and government. These men were commissioned by the General Assembly to revise, or alter, or to recommend repeal or to introduce all or any of the laws of Virginia, although the work of the Committee of course did not have the force and effect of state law until passed by the General Assembly.

The next four days were busy and momentous ones for this group. From this meeting evolved the Statute of Religious Freedom which was authored by Thomas Jefferson. In his evaluation of this immortal document Dumas Malone, celebrated biographer of Thomas Jefferson, wrote in his sketch on Jefferson in the Dictionary of American Biography:

"In its assertion that the mind is not subject to coercion, the civil rights have no dependence on religious opinions and the opinions of men are not the concern of civil government, it is indeed one of the great American charters of freedom."

Jefferson himself valued his Fredericksburg project among the three most important accomplishments of his incredibly productive career. He wrote

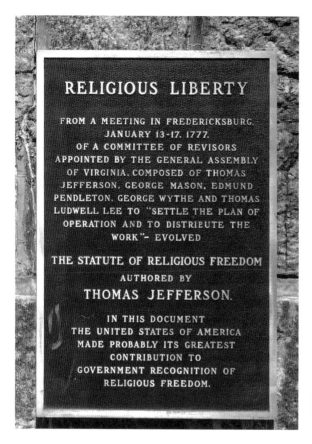

Religious Freedom
Monument plaque. *Allen
Browne, landmarks.*

*his own epitaph, which many of you have seen on his tomb at Monticello
and he wanted to be remembered only for having been the author of the
Declaration of American Independence, and of the Statute of Virginia for
Religious Freedom and as the father of the University of Virginia.*

*With the strong backing of James Madison (and he deserves tremendous
credit) the Bill for Religious Freedom finally passed the Virginia General
Assembly on January 16, 1786. Jefferson, as we have seen, ranked it with
the Declaration of Independence and considered it a natural sequence of it.
As the Declaration of Independence "asserted the natural right of a people
to choose any form of government conductive to their safety and happiness,"
so the Bill for Establishing Religious Freedom asserted the natural right of
a person to choose his beliefs and opinions free of compulsion.*

*The full text as drafted by Jefferson was printed six years before its
slightly altered version was enacted into law. Actually, Jefferson was
in France at the time of its enactment and praised Madison and other*

compatriots for their unremitting efforts to have it passed as a Virginia Statute and he saw to it that its passage received worldwide attention and distribution. In a letter to Madison in 1786, following the passage of the Act, he wrote:

"It is honorable for us to have produced the first legislature who had the courage to declare that the reason of man may be trusted with the formation of his opinions."

The earliest known printed text of this landmark Statute is found in a broadside, or hand bill preserved at the Boston Public Library. The Preamble is long and gives an exhaustive statement of Jefferson's personal and political philosophy, very readable and well worth studying and digesting, but the thrust of the Act states in one sentence that:

"We the General Assembly of Virginia do enact that no man shall be compelled to frequent or support any religious worship, place, or ministry whatsoever, nor shall be enforced, restrained, molested, or burthened in his body or goods, nor shall otherwise suffer, on account of his religious opinions or belief; but that all men shall be free to profess, and by argument to maintain, their opinions in matters of religion, and that the same shall in no wise diminish, enlarge, or affect their civil capacities."

We must remember that at that time religion was almost synonymous with the Church of England, of which Virginia was a colony, and which church was maintained as an arm of government, and that some of the edicts of the church in many phases of life had the force and effect of law.

At the time the proposed Statute of Religious Freedom was being drafted in Fredericksburg, no doubt numerous members of the gentry took advantage of their opportunity to spend some relaxing hours with the group at the Tavern and in showing them the sights of the town, following which they were offered the hospitality of the homes of Fredericksburg. Mann Page, a well-known Fredericksburg citizen of that day, made his coach with driver available to visit the sights of the town and to see the gunnery and the weaving mill, two thriving industries. These and other personal activities were recorded by Thomas Jefferson in his account book, now in the Alderman Library in the University of Virginia.

An interesting bit of trivia therein not only definitely established where the group stayed during its historic meeting but covered some items of his expenses, including on January 13th his visit to the barber and his having his watch mended. There would seem little doubt that the barber he referred to was the wig maker and barber John Atkinson whose shop was located a short distance down Caroline Street from Weedon's Tavern on the southwest corner of George and Caroline. These small mundane items show us that life in those days was not so different in some ways from that of today. Yet, a dramatic moment in the modern history of mankind was occurring here on this very soil, and a yearning hope of oppressed humanity was taking early shape.

Those of us in Fredericksburg and especially those here today commemorating that great event owe a lasting debt of gratitude to Dr. Leidecker and to the Thomas Jefferson Institute for the Study of Religious Freedom which sponsors the annual gathering of this small band of modern day patriots to whom I extend a warm and heartfelt salute!

In 2003, Supreme Court justice Antonin Scalia, in his address to the gathered public for this ceremony, said, "Government will not favor Catholics, Protestants, Muslims, Jews. But the tradition was never that the government had to be neutral between religiousness and non-religiousness. Court decisions forbidding mentions of God in public events are the result of interpretations of the Constitution that are too elastic."

At the 2007 ceremony, Virginia House speaker Bill Howell told the crowd, "It is no mistake that the right to religious freedom is in the First Amendment....Religious freedom preceded those other freedoms because, without it, no freedom can exist." He also said the "Statute of Religious Freedom gives us the freedom *of* religion, not *from* religion."

In 2009, Representative Rob Wittman, First District congressman of Virginia, said of Jefferson, "He made it his life's work to make sure we preserved our religious freedoms, and we understood the need for protecting our natural rights, those given to us by God."

The 2014 Religious Freedom Day celebration was met with criticism.

As customary sponsors, the Knights of Columbus dominated the parade, adorned in feathered hats, swords and capes. Following closely behind the Knights of Columbus was a local Boy Scout troop, who were then followed by representatives from a local Lutheran church with their banner, then a small group of Muslims from the Fredericksburg Ummah Islamic Center, the Fredericksburg Coalition of Reason (CoR), the Washington Area Secular Humanists and, finally, the Unitarian Universalist (UU) Fellowship of Fredericksburg.

The UU and Fredericksburg CoR groups were invited to stand nearer to the platform with their banners. The platform was filled with an array of about forty-five dignitaries—twenty-five of whom were Knights, at least three of whom were Masons, more than five of whom were Christian leaders, three were Muslims and the remainder were various elected officials.

Virginia delegate Robert D. Orrock was the master of ceremonies and opened the festivities with the Pledge of Allegiance. Orrock remained adamant about the use of the phrase "under God," as he explained that the term was as the pledge is written.

Following a heavily theistic prayer delivered by Reverend Lawrence Davies (the former mayor of Fredericksburg), the Honorable Mayor Mary Katherine Greenlaw provided the historical backdrop to the importance of the commemoration. Former Virginia attorney general Ken Cuccinelli gave the keynote address.

Critics asked why there wasn't a more diverse range of belief groups—including nontheistic—represented on the platform and why, in light of religious liberty, nobody asked the Sheikh Imam to offer a Muslim du'a, despite being only a few feet behind the podium.

To see real religious liberty, one would have needed to attend the event after the parade, cosponsored by Fredericksburg CoR and the University of Mary Washington. There, three students—self-professed and unashamed Christians—were given cash awards for their essays on why religious liberty for everyone is important to them.

Since 1993, Religious Freedom Day has also been commemorated nationally on January 16 via a proclamation by the president of the United States.

The first official proclamation was given by President George H. Bush on December 9, 1992, declaring Religious Freedom Day. In it, he acknowledged our debt to Thomas Jefferson:

> *We Americans have long cherished our identity as one Nation under God. To this day American law and institutions have been shaped by a view of man that recognizes the inherent rights and dignity of individuals. The Framers of our Government shared this view, and they never forgot the political and religious persecution that had forced their ancestors to flee Europe. Thus, it is not surprising that the first of all freedoms enumerated in our Bill of Rights is freedom of religion. The first amendment to our Constitution states that "Congress shall make no law respecting an establishment of religion, or prohibiting the free exercise thereof."*

As we reflect on our Constitution and Bill of Rights, we do well to acknowledge our debt to Thomas Jefferson and James Madison. These two men were instrumental in establishing the American tradition of religious liberty and tolerance. Thomas Jefferson articulated the idea of religious liberty in his 1777 draft Bill for Establishing Religious Freedom in Virginia. In that bill, he wrote:

"All men shall be free to profess, and by argument to maintain, their opinion in matters of religion, and that the same shall in no wise…affect their civil capacities."

James Madison later introduced and championed this bill in the Virginia House of Delegates, where it passed in 1786. Following the Federal Constitutional Convention of 1787, James Madison led the way in drafting our Bill of Rights.

The religious freedom that James Madison and Thomas Jefferson helped to secure for us has been integral to the preservation and development of the United States. Over the years the exercise of our religious freedom has been instrumental in preserving the faith and the traditional values that are this Nation's greatest strengths. Moreover, the free exercise of religion goes hand in hand with the preservation of our other rights. As Thomas Jefferson noted, the first amendment "guards in the same sentence, and under the same words, the freedom of religion, of speech, and of the press; insomuch as that whatever violates either throws down the sanctuary which covers the others." That sanctuary is the spirit of life, liberty, truth, and justice.

In that spirit, the United States has continued to champion religious liberty and tolerance around the world. We decry as reprehensible the persecution of ethnic and religious minorities, and we likewise condemn the resurgence of anti-Semitism and other forms of religious bigotry. The United States calls on all nations to respect the fundamental rights of individuals, in accordance with international human rights agreements and in recognition of the direct and inexorable relationship between freedom and justice and the achievement of lasting peace in the world.

The Congress, by House Joint Resolution 457, has designated January 16, 1993, as "Religious Freedom Day" and has requested the President to issue a proclamation in observance of this day.

Now, Therefore, I, George Bush, President of the United States of America, do hereby proclaim January 16, 1993, as Religious Freedom Day. I urge all Americans to observe this day with appropriate ceremonies and activities in their homes, schools, and places of worship as an expression of our gratitude for the blessings of liberty and as a sign of our resolve to protect and preserve them.

In Witness Whereof, I have hereunto set my hand this ninth day of December, in the year of our Lord nineteen hundred and ninety-two, and of the Independence of the United States of America the two hundred and seventeenth.

George Bush

The congressional resolution that established Religious Freedom Day reads, in part:

Whereas the first amendment to the Constitution of the United States guarantees religious liberty to the people of the United States;

Whereas millions of people from all parts of the world have come to the United States fleeing religious persecution and seeking freedom to worship;

Whereas in 1777 Thomas Jefferson wrote the bill entitled "A Bill for Establishing Religious Freedom in Virginia" to guarantee freedom of conscience and separation of church and state;

Whereas in 1786, through the devotion of Virginians such as George Mason and James Madison, the General Assembly of Virginia passed such bill;

Whereas the Statute of Virginia for Religious Freedom inspired and shaped the guarantees of religious freedom in the first amendment;

Whereas the Supreme Court of the United States has recognized repeatedly that the Statute of Virginia for Religious Freedom was an important influence in the development of the Bill of Rights.

A diverse group of more than seventy-five religious and civil society leaders came together to sign the American Charter of Freedom of Religion and Conscience. Article 1 of the charter states:

[Religious] *freedom is a bedrock of personal liberty, a safeguard for communal freedom, and a wellspring of social pluralism. It assumes diversity in matters of belief and stands against enforced coercions, whether religious, ideological, political, or social. As well as protecting the freedom of the "inner forum" of the mind and conscience, this right protects the freedom of the "outer forum" of the nation's public square. From Thomas*

Jefferson's avowal that "Almighty God hath created the mind free," to the Rev. Dr. Martin Luther King Jr.'s insistence that the church "is not the master or the servant of the state, but rather the conscience of the state," our greatest leaders have affirmed that fulfilling humankind's highest potential and responsibilities requires that individuals and communities be free to exercise their convictions of conscience in every arena of life. Freedom of religion and conscience is a foundational and inalienable liberty held by every human being in equal measure. To treat it as anything less, or to restrict it for any but the most pressing reasons, is to undermine human dignity, human rights, and equality.

Article 13 of the *charter* states:

In a nation of profound diversity, freedom of religion and conscience is best secured through a civil public square. A "civil public square" is an arena of public life in which all people are free to enter and engage on the basis of their ultimate beliefs, but always under the canopy of the American covenant as embodied in the U.S. Constitution. This covenant includes people of all ultimate beliefs, religious and secularist, and sets forth the understanding of what is just, liberal, and empowering for all. The practical implications of this covenant are twofold. First, the rights

Thomas Jefferson's sixth-great-grandson Shannon LaNier. *Drew Gardner.*

of all people are to be respected equally and according to the rule of law. Second, in accordance with our understanding that freedom of religion and conscience depends on a freely agreed covenant, all people must respect the rights of all others and strive in good faith to negotiate differences civilly and peacefully. Such a covenant is moral and political. It does not attempt to ground unity and civility in enforced conformity concerning the substance of particular religious or secular doctrines. Rather, this covenant secures unity and civility on the basis of voluntary agreement on foundational moral and political principles—principles of human dignity and human rights.

A recognition of Jefferson's efforts is also conducted each March. Since 2002, the 225th anniversary of the writing of this work, the Department of Classics, Philosophy and Religion at the University of Mary Washington has sponsored the annual "Jefferson Lecture on Religious Freedom." The lecture brings to the campus and community a wide range of public figures and distinguished scholars to discuss the nature and importance of religious freedom and the legacy of Jefferson's statute. In 2022, "Jefferson's Children: The Story of One American Family" featured Shannon LaNier, the president's sixth-great-grandson, as its keynote speaker. LaNier was descended from Jefferson and an enslaved woman named Sally Hemmings.

13

JEFFERSON'S LEGACY

Truth is great and will prevail if left to herself; she is the proper and sufficient
antagonist to error, and has nothing to fear from the conflict
unless by human interposition.
—Jefferson Memorial in Washington

Jefferson is remembered as the founding father whose writing contributions
shaped the United States. His works championing values such as freedom
of ideas, speech and religion inspired the Revolution and led to American
independence. As the author of the Declaration of Independence and
the Virginia Statute for Religious Freedom, which directly influenced the
U.S. Constitution, Jefferson has had his words inscribed on the walls of the
foundation of the country he helped create.

Presidential scholars and historians generally praise his achievements,
including his advocacy of religious freedom and tolerance in Virginia. He
was also a proponent of democracy, republicanism and individual rights.

As president, Jefferson often communicated with representatives of
religious organizations and reaffirmed his dedication to religious liberty. In a
letter to George Outlaw, he wrote:

Washington
June 24. 1806.
Sir
I have duly received the Address signed by yourself on behalf of the
Ministers & Messengers of the several Baptist churches of the North

Jefferson Memorial statue, by Carol. M. Highsmith, 1946. *Library of Congress.*

Carolina Chowan association held at Salem, and I proffer my thanks for the favorable sentiments which it expresses towards myself personally. The happiness which our country enjoys in the pursuits of peace and industry ought to endear that course to all it's [sic] citizens, and to kindle their hearts with gratitude to the being under whose providence these blessings are held.

we owe to him especial thanks for the right we enjoy to worship him, every one [sic] in his own way, and that we have been singled out to prove by experience the innocence of freedom in religious opinions & exercises, the power of reason to maintain itself against error, and the comfort of living under laws which assure us that in these things "there is none who shall make us afraid."

I am peculiarly gratified by the confidence you express that no attempt will ever be made by me to violate the trust reposed in me by my fellow citizens, or to endanger their happiness. in this confidence you shall never be disappointed. my heart never felt a wish unfriendly to the general good of my fellow-citizens.

Be so kind as to present my thanks to the churches of your association, & to assure them of my prayers for the continuance of every blessing to them now & hereafter: and accept yourself my salutations & assurances of great respect & consideration.

Th: Jefferson

Jefferson is regarded as a leading spokesman for democracy and republicanism in the era of the Enlightenment. He was also a Renaissance man. Primarily a planter, lawyer and politician who mastered many disciplines, which ranged from surveying and mathematics to horticulture and mechanics, Jefferson was also an architect in the classical tradition. He maintained a keen interest in religion and philosophy, which influenced much of his perspective on life. A philologist, he knew several languages. He was a prolific letter writer and corresponded with many prominent people.

Jefferson served the public most of his life: first as the second governor of Virginia from 1779 to 1781 and then as the United States minister to France in May 1785, the first secretary of state from 1790 to 1793, the second vice president of the United States from 1797 to 1801 and as the third president of the United States from 1801 to 1809.

According to the *Encyclopedia of American Politics*, Jefferson's life was full of many significant events:

1743: Born on April 13 in Virginia.
1760: Enrolled at William and Mary College at Williamsburg at the age of sixteen.
1762: Graduated from William and Mary College.
1768: Elected to the House of Burgesses.
1772: Married Martha Wayles Skelton.

1774: Wrote *A Summary View of the Rights of British America*.
1775: Elected to the Continental Congress.
1776: Wrote the Declaration of Independence.
1777: Authored the Virginia Statute for Religious Freedom.
1779: Elected as the second governor of Virginia.
1784: Appointed as the minister to France.
1790: Became the first secretary of state.
1796: Elected vice president of the United States.
1801: Elected president of the United States.
1803: The United States purchased the Louisiana Territory from France for $15 million.
1805: Lewis and Clark, sent on an expedition by Jefferson, reached the Pacific coast.
1807: Arron Burr, Jefferson's vice president, was tried and acquitted for treason.
1807: Congress prohibited the importation of enslaved people from Africa to the United States.
1809: Retired from public life.
1819: Founded the University of Virginia.
1826: Died on July 4 at his home, Monticello.

Jefferson's time in Fredericksburg in 1777 resulted in one of the most significant documents ever put forth in the annals of this country's history. His selection of the small yet bustling town on the banks of the Rappahannock River says much for its welcoming atmosphere. The January days the committee spent at the tavern, contemplating the fulfillment of their task while taking time to enjoy their surroundings, says much for the hospitality of the town. The fact that Jefferson was a visitor on more than one occasion reinforces his affinity for the city and its people. The legacy he left behind, as part of the city's history, is both remarkable and memorable.

The following is a timeline of events:

June 12, 1776: The Virginia Convention adopts the Declaration of Rights, including the sixteenth article, which guarantees citizens the "free exercise of religion."

October 1776–December 1776: Thomas Jefferson and James Madison successfully advocate for "an act for exempting the different societies of Dissenters from contributing to the support and maintenance of the church as by law established, and its ministers, and for other purposes therein mentioned."

January 13–17, 1777: Thomas Jefferson travels to Fredericksburg and drafts a bill "for establishing religious freedom" as part of an effort to revise Virginia's colonial laws in order to remove vestiges of monarchy and align them more closely with the state's republican principles and its new independent status.

June 12, 1779: Because Thomas Jefferson had since been elected governor, John Harvie introduces Jefferson's bill "for establishing religious freedom" to the House of Delegates. It is eventually tabled.

November 11, 1784: The House of Delegates adopts a resolution supporting "a moderate tax or contribution, annually" to benefit all Christian sects. The resolution eventually fails.

June 20, 1785: James Madison anonymously authors his *Memorial and Remonstrance Against Religious Assessments*, a broadside in opposition to a resolution by the House of Delegates to levy a general assessment to benefit all Christian sects.

October 31, 1785: James Madison reintroduces to the House of Burgesses 117 bills from an earlier effort to revise Virginia's laws. Among these is Thomas Jefferson's bill "for establishing religious freedom."

January 16, 1786: The general assembly passes the Bill for Establishing Religious Freedom. Written by Thomas Jefferson and championed in the House of Delegates by James Madison, the bill effectively severs the connection between church and state.

Viewed historically, the Virginia Statute for Religious Freedom is the ultimate expression of enlightenment in the life and work of Thomas Jefferson. The statute was Jefferson's intellectual effort to dismiss "spiritual tyranny." He certainly succeeded in his goal.

Nowhere in the world today is there more genuine freedom of conscience and more respect for the separateness of church and state than there is in the United States of America. Jefferson's statute laid the foundation for the unique American experience of religious liberty. Philip Schaff, a German theologian, studied the matter and concluded the following:

> *The vitality of religion* [in America] *is owing to its self-reliance, its freedom, and its abstention from politics. The voluntary system develops individual activity and liberality in the support of religion, while the state-church system has the opposite effect.*

Jefferson Memorial. *Washington, D.C.*

Fittingly, words from the Virginia Statute for Religious Freedom are among those that line the walls of the Jefferson Memorial in Washington, D.C. Its remarkable dome on the north portico is inscribed by his own dedication:

> *Almighty God hath created the mind free. All attempts to influence it by temporal punishments or burthens…are a departure from the plan of the holy Author of our religion.….No man shall be compelled to frequent or support religious worship or ministry or shall otherwise suffer on account of his religious opinions or belief, but all men shall be free to profess and by argument to maintain, their opinions in matters of religion. I know but one code of morality for men whether acting singly or collectively.*

Appendix A

COMMITTEE OF REVISORS

We have the honor to be with the utmost respect, Sir,
Your most obedient And most humble servants.
—Thomas Jefferson

The Committee of Revisors, in addition to Jefferson, was tasked with addressing the Virginia laws. The committee included:

George Wythe lithograph, 1876. *Library of Congress.*

GEORGE WYTHE: In addition to serving as one of Virginia's representatives to the Continental Congress and the Philadelphia Convention, Wythe was one of the signatories of the Declaration of Independence. As a member of the House of Burgesses, he helped oversee wartime expenditures during the French and Indian War. Wythe also opposed the Stamp Act and other taxes from England that were imposed on the colonies. He was a prominent law professor at the prestigious College of William and Mary. Wythe became increasingly troubled by the institution of slavery and emancipated all of his enslaved people following the victory of the American Revolution. This was viewed as an unusual move among wealthy Virginians who depended on enslaved labor. In his will, Wythe left his large book collection to Jefferson. This was part of the collection Jefferson later sold to establish the Library of Congress. He refused an offer to take possession of Wythe's lecture notes and legal papers, rather recommending that they be donated to the Library of Virginia. Jefferson's grandson George Wythe Randolph was named after Wythe.

EDMUND PENDLETON: He served in the Virginia legislature before and during the Revolutionary War and became the first speaker of the Virginia House of Delegates. Pendleton attended the First Continental Congress as one of Virginia's delegates, signed the Continental Association and led the conventions when Virginia declared and adopted the U.S. Constitution. Pendleton served as president of the Virginia Committee of Safety and as president of the Virginia Convention that authorized Virginia's delegates to propose a resolution to break from England and create a Declaration of Independence.

Edmund Pendleton
by William L. Marcy Pendleton. Scvahistory.

Unlike Wythe, Pendleton proposed the modification in the statement of universal rights in Virginia's declaration to exclude the enslaved, thus winning support of his fellow enslavers. Delegates unanimously selected Pendleton as president of the Virginia Ratifying Convention. When a Supreme Court of Appeals was established in Virginia, Pendleton was appointed as its first president.

GEORGE MASON: He authored the first draft of the Virginia Declaration of Rights, and his words formed much of the text adopted by the final Virginia Convention. He also wrote a constitution for the state. Jefferson and others tried to have the convention adopt their ideas, but they found that Mason's efforts could not be stopped. During the Revolutionary War, Mason was a member of the House of Delegates of Virginia's General Assembly. Surprisingly, he refused to serve in the Continental Congress. Mason was named one of his state's delegates to the Constitutional Convention. Several of the clauses in the Constitution were due to his

George Mason Portrait.
From the Encyclopedia of Virginia.

efforts. He was active in the convention for months before deciding he could not sign it. He cited the lack of a bill of rights as the primary cause. Mason wanted to end the slave trade and a supermajority requirement for navigation acts, fearing that restrictions on shipping might harm his state of Virginia. He failed to attain these goals.

Thomas Ludwell Lee: Lee was born into the wealthy Lee family of Virginia. Stafford County, Virginia voters elected Lee as one of their delegates to the House of Burgesses and he won re-election. Lee was later made a member of the Virginia Senate. He continued his political involvement as one of Stafford County's representatives to the Third, Fourth and Fifth Virginia Conventions. He may be best known as one of the editors of the Virginia Declaration of Rights. After Virginia established its own constitution, Lee was elected to the Virginia Senate to represent the Northern Neck of Virginia and King George, Stafford and Westmoreland Counties. Lee was a founding member of the Mississippi Company, which attempted to purchase property in modern-day Tennessee and Kentucky. Unfortunately, the Proclamation of 1763 prohibited their investor's goal of separating the colonial's territory from the Native Americans. Since Virginians had just participated in the French and Indian War with the hopes of procuring this land, the proclamation influenced the beginning of the Revolutionary War.

The revision of the Virginia laws that Jefferson and the four other participants originally embarked on, with the exception of the Bill for Establishing Religious Freedom, faded into obscurity. This is chiefly because the revision of the laws itself never came into emphasis and never materialized in a single presentation, as in the case of earlier revisions in Virginia. The encompassing goal of the revision, extending over a full decade, would have been buried, even without such an importance on some of its parts. There is no manuscript in existence for the entire "Report of the Committee of Revisors," meaning no formal report was submitted to the general assembly. The result was nothing more than ordinary legislation in the decade between 1776 and 1786, with an occasional landmark standing out. Jefferson and Wythe, with Pendleton's concurrence, addressed this factor, explaining the committee's efforts in their letter to Benjamin Harrison:

> *Williamsburg, June 18, 1779*
> *Sir*
> *The committee appointed in pursuance of an act of General Assembly passed in 1776, intituled "An act for the revision of the laws," have*

according to the requisitions of the said act gone through that work, and prepared 126 bills, the titles of which are stated in the inclosed [sic] catalogue. Some of these bills have been presented to the House of Delegates in the course of the present session two or three of them delivered to members of that House at their request to be presented, the rest are in the two bundles which accompany this; these we take the liberty through you of presenting to the General Assembly.

In the course of this work we were unfortunately deprived of the assistance and abilities of two of our associates appointed by the General Assembly, of the one by death, of the other by resignation. As the plan of the work had been settled, and agreeable to that plan it was in a considerable degree carried into execution before that loss, we did not exercise the powers given us by the act, of filling up the places by new appointments, being desirous that the plan agreed on by members who were specially appointed by the Assembly, might not be liable to alteration from others who might not equally possess their confidence, it has therefore been executed by the three remaining members, one of whom being prevented from putting his signature hereto, by the great distance of his residence from this city, has by letter authorized us to declare his concurrence in the report.

We have the honor to be with the utmost respect, Sir, Your most obedient And most humble servants,

T. Jefferson,
G. Wythe.

The most contemporaneous account of the revisions can be found in Jefferson's *Notes on Virginia*. It includes a fairly accurate index of what Jefferson considered to be his own important contributions to the endeavor. Jefferson was clearly unimpressed with the results. He wrote to G.K. van Hogendorp, "It contains not more than three or four laws which could strike the attention of a foreigner.…The only merit of this work is that it may remove from our book shelves about twenty folio volumes of statutes, retaining all the parts of them which either their own merit or the established system of laws required."

In his *Notes on Virginia*, Jefferson remarked on the committee's accomplishments that he deemed worth commenting on. He wrote this:

Many of the laws which were in force during the monarchy being relative merely to that form of government, or inculcating principles inconsistent with republicanism, the first assembly which met after the establishment of the commonwealth appointed a committee to revise the whole code, to reduce it into proper 143 form and volume, and report it to the assembly. This work has been executed by three gentlemen, and reported; but probably will not be taken up till a restoration of peace shall leave to the legislature leisure to go through such a work.

The plan of the revisal was this. The common law of England, by which is meant, that part of the English law which was anterior to the date of the oldest statutes extant, is made the basis of the work. It was thought dangerous to attempt to reduce it to a text: it was therefore left to be collected from the usual monuments of it. Necessary alterations in that, and so much of the whole body of the British statutes, and of acts of assembly, as were thought proper to be retained, were digested into 126 new acts, in which simplicity of style was aimed at, as far as was safe.

The following are the most remarkable alterations proposed:

To change the rules of descent, so as that the lands of any person dying intestate shall be divisible equally among all his children, or other representatives, in equal degree.

To make slaves distributable among the next of kin, as other moveables.

To have all public expenses, whether of the general treasury, or of a parish or county supplied by assessments on the citizens, in proportion to their property.

To hire undertakers for keeping the public roads in repair, and indemnify individuals through whose lands new roads shall be opened.

To define with precision the rules whereby aliens should become citizens, and citizens make themselves aliens.

To establish religious freedom on the broadest bottom.

To emancipate all slaves born after passing the act.

JEFFERSON QUOTES ON RELIGIOUS FREEDOM

"The law for religious freedom…put down the aristocracy of the clergy, and restored to the citizen the freedom of the mind."

"The clergy, by getting themselves established by law, & ingrafted into the machine of government, have been a very formidable engine against the civil & religious rights of man."

"On the subject of religion, a subject on which I have ever been most scrupulously reserved. I have considered it as a matter between every man and his maker, in which no other, & far less the public, had a right to intermeddle."

"Believing with you that religion is a matter which lies solely between Man & his God, that he owes account to none other for his faith or his worship, that the legitimate powers of government reach actions only, & not opinions, I contemplate with sovereign reverence that act of the whole American people which declared that their legislature should 'make no law respecting an establishment of religion, or prohibiting the free exercise thereof,' thus building a wall of separation between Church & State."

"If the freedom of religion, guaranteed to us by law in theory, can ever rise in practice under the overbearing inquisition of public opinion, truth will prevail over fanaticism, and the genuine doctrines of Jesus, so long perverted by His pseudo-priests, will again be restored to their original purity. This reformation will advance with the other improvements of the human mind."

Jefferson steel engraving by Stuart Gilbert. *Library of Congress.*

"But our rulers can have authority over such natural rights only as we have submitted to them. The rights of conscience we never submitted, we could not submit. We are answerable for them to our God. The legitimate powers of government extend to such acts only as are injurious to others. But it does me no injury for my neighbour to say there are twenty gods, or no god. It neither picks my pocket nor breaks my leg. ...Reason and free enquiry are the only effectual agents against error."

"I must ever believe that religion substantially good which produces an honest life, and we have been authorised [sic] *by one, whom you and I equally respect, to judge of the tree by it's* [sic] *fruit our particular principles of religion are a subject of accountability to our god alone. I enquire after no man's, and trouble none with mine: nor is it given to us in this life to know whether your's* [sic] *or mine, our friend's or our foe's are exactly the right."*

"The bill for establishing religious freedom, the principles of which had, to a certain degree, been enacted before, I had drawn in all the latitude of reason & right. it still met with opposition; but, with some mutilations in the preamble, it was finally past; and a singular proposition proved that it's protection of opinion was meant to be universal where the preamble declares that coercion is a departure from the plan of the holy author of our religion, an amendment was proposed, by inserting the words 'Jesus Christ' so that it should read 'a departure from the plan of Jesus Christ, the holy author of our religion' the insertion was rejected by a great majority, in proof that they meant to comprehend, within the mantle of it's [sic] *protection, the Jew and the Gentile, the Christian and Mahometan, the Hindoo* [sic] *and infidel of every denomination."*

"Th: Jefferson returns his thanks…for the eloquent discourse on the Consecration of the Synagogue of Savannah…it excites in him the gratifying reflection that his own country has been the first to prove to the world two truths, the most salutary to human society, that man can govern himself, and that religious freedom is the most effectual Anodyne against religious dissension."

"Our citizens have wisely formed themselves into one nation as to others, and several states as among themselves to the United nation belongs our external & mutual relations: to each state severally the care of our persons, our property, our reputation, and religious freedom. this wise distribution, if carefully preserved, will prove I trust, from example, that while smaller governments are better adapted to the ordinary objects of society, larger confederations more effectually secure independence, and the preservation of republican government."

BILL NO. 82, A BILL FOR ESTABLISHING RELIGIOUS FREEDOM

Well aware that the opinions and belief of men depend not on their own will, but follow involuntarily the evidence proposed to their minds; that Almighty God hath created the mind free, and manifested his supreme will that free it shall remain by making it altogether insusceptible of restraint; that all attempts to influence it by temporal punishments, or burthens, or by civil incapacitations, tend only to beget habits of hypocrisy and meanness, and are a departure from the plan of the holy author of our religion, who being lord both of body and mind, yet chose not to propagate it by coercions on either, as was in his Almighty power to do, but to extend it by its influence on reason alone; that the impious presumption of legislators and rulers, civil as well as ecclesiastical, who, being themselves but fallible and uninspired men, have assumed dominion over the faith of others, setting up their own opinions and modes of thinking as the only true and infallible, and as such endeavoring to impose them on others, hath established and maintained false religions over the greatest part of the world and through all time: That to compel a man to furnish contributions of money for the propagation of opinions which he disbelieves and abhors, is sinful and tyrannical; that even the forcing him to support this or that teacher of his own religious persuasion, is depriving him of the comfortable liberty of giving his contributions to the particular pastor whose morals he would make his pattern, and whose powers he feels most persuasive to righteousness; and is withdrawing from the ministry those temporary rewards, which proceeding from an approbation of their personal conduct, are an additional incitement to earnest and unremitting labours for the instruction of mankind; that our civil rights have no dependance on our religious opinions, any more than our opinions in physics or geometry; that therefore the proscribing any citizen as unworthy the public confidence by laying upon him an incapacity of being called to offices of trust and emolument, unless he profess or renounce this or that religious opinion, is depriving him injuriously of those privileges and advantages to which, in common with his fellow citizens, he has a natural right; that it tends also to corrupt the principles of that very religion it is meant to encourage, by bribing, with a monopoly of worldly honours and emoluments, those who will externally profess and conform to it; that though indeed these are criminal who do not withstand such temptation, yet neither are those innocent who lay the bait in their way; that the opinions of men are not the object of civil government, nor under its jurisdiction; that to suffer the civil magistrate to intrude his powers into the field of opinion and to restrain the profession or propagation of principles on supposition of their ill tendency is a dangerous falacy [sic], which at once destroys all religious liberty, because he being of course judge of that tendency will make his opinions the rule of judgment, and approve or condemn the sentiments of others only as they shall square with or differ from his own; that it is time enough for the rightful purposes of civil government for its officers to interfere when principles break out into overt acts against peace and good order; and finally, that truth is great and will prevail if left to herself; that she is the proper and sufficient antagonist to error, and has nothing to fear from the conflict unless by human interposition disarmed of her natural weapons, free argument and debate; errors ceasing to be dangerous when it is permitted freely to contradict them.

We the General Assembly of Virginia do enact that no man shall be compelled to frequent or support any religious worship, place, or ministry whatsoever, nor shall be enforced, restrained, molested, or burthened in his body or goods, nor shall otherwise suffer, on account of his religious opinions or belief; but that all men shall be free to profess, and by argument to maintain, their opinions in matters of religion, and that the same shall in no wise diminish, enlarge, or affect their civil capacities.

And though we well know that this Assembly, elected by the people for the ordinary purposes of legislation only, have no power to restrain the acts of succeeding Assemblies, constituted with powers equal to our own, and that therefore to declare this act irrevocable would be of no effect in law; yet we are free to declare, and do declare, that the rights hereby asserted are of the natural rights of mankind, and that if any act shall be hereafter passed to repeal the present or to narrow its operation, such act will be an infringement of natural right.

Appendix D

ADDITIONAL LETTERS

To Francis Adrian Van der Kemp (explaining *The Jefferson Bible*):

Poplar Forest near Lynchburg Apr. 25. 16.
Sir
Your favor of Mar. 24. was handed to me just as I was setting out on a journey of time and distance, which will explain the date of this both as to time and place. the Syllabus, which is the subject of your letter, was addressed to a friend to whom I had promised a more detailed view. but finding I should never have time for that, I sent him what I thought should be the Outlines of such a work. the same subject entering sometimes into the correspondence between mr Adams and myself, I sent him a copy of it. the friend to whom it had been first addressed dying soon after, I asked from his family the return of the original, as a confidential communication, which they kindly sent me. so that no copy of it, but that in possession of mr Adams, now exists out of my own hands. I have used this caution, lest it should get out in connection with my name; and I was unwilling to draw on myself a swarm of insects, whose buz [sic] is more disquieting than their bite. as an abstract thing, and without any intimation from what quarter derived, I can have no objection to it's [sic] being committed to the consideration of the world. I believe it may even do good by producing discussion, and finally a true view of the merits of this great reformer. pursuing the same ideas after writing the Syllabus, I made, for my own satisfaction, an Extract from the Evangelists of the texts of his morals,

selecting those only whose style and spirit proved them genuine, and his own: and they are as distinguishable from the matter in which they are imbedded as diamonds in dunghills. a more precious morsel of ethics was never seen. it was too hastily done however, being the work of one or two evenings only, while I lived at Washington, overwhelmed with other business: and it is my intention to go over it again at more leisure. this shall be the work of the ensuing winter. I gave it the title of "the Philosophy of Jesus extracted from the text of the Evangelists." to this Syllabus and Extract, if a history of his life can be added, written with the same view of the subject, the world will see, after the fogs shall be dispelled, in which for 14. centuries he has been inveloped [sic] by Jugglers to make money of him, when the genuine character shall be exhibited, which they have dressed up in the rags of an Impostor. the world, I say, will at length see the immortal merit of this first of human Sages. I rejoice that you think of undertaking this work. it is one I have long wished to see written on the scale of a Laertius or a Nepos. nor can it be a work of labor, or of volume. for his journeyings from Judaea to Samaria, and Samaria to Galilee, do not cover much country; and the incidents of his life require little research. they are all at hand, and need only to be put into human dress; noticing such only as are within the physical laws of nature, and offending none by a denial, or even a mention, of what is not. if the Syllabus and Extract (which is short) either in substance, or at large, are worth a place under the same cover with your biography, they are at your service. I ask one only condition, that no possibility shall be admitted of my name being even intimated with the publication. if done in England, as you seem to contemplate, there will be the less likelihood of my being thought of. I shall be much gratified to learn that you pursue your intention of writing the life of Jesus, and pray to accept the assurances of my great respect and esteem.
Th: Jefferson

To John Adams (on the existence of God):

Monticello April 11. 23.
Dear Sir
The wishes expressed, in your last favor, that I may continue in life and health until I become a Calvinist, at least in his exclamation of "mon Dieu! jusque à quand!" *would make me immortal. I can never join Calvin in addressing his god. he was indeed an Atheist, which I can never be; or rather his religion was Dæmonism. if ever man worshipped a false*

god, he did. the being described in his 5. points is not the God whom you and I acknolege [sic] *and adore, the Creator and benevolent governor of the world; but a dæmon of malignant spirit. it would be more pardonable to believe in no god at all, than to blaspheme him by the atrocious attributes of Calvin. indeed I think that every Christian sect gives a great handle to Atheism by their general dogma that, without a revelation, there would not be sufficient proof of the being of a god. now one sixth of mankind only are supposed to be Christians: the other five sixths then, who do not believe in the Jewish and Christian revelation, are without a knolege* [sic] *of the existence of a god! this gives compleatly* [sic] *a gain de cause to the disciples of Ocellus, Timaeus, Spinosa, Diderot and D'Holbach. the argument which they rest on as triumphant and unanswerable is that, in every hypothesis of Cosmogony you must admit an eternal pre-existence of something; and according to the rule of sound philosophy, you are never to employ two principles to solve a difficulty when one will suffice. they say then that it is more simple to believe at once in the eternal pre-existence of the world, as it is now going on, and may for ever go on by the principle of reproduction which we see and witness, than to believe in the eternal pre-existence of an ulterior cause, or Creator of the world, a being whom we see not, and know not, of whose form substance and mode or place of existence, or of action no sense informs us, no power of the mind enables us to delineate or comprehend. on the contrary I hold (without appeal to revelation) that when we take a view of the Universe, in it's* [sic] *parts general or particular, it is impossible for the human mind not to percieve* [sic] *and feel a conviction of design, consummate skill, and indefinite power in every atom of it's* [sic] *composition. the movements of the heavenly bodies, so exactly held in their course by the balance of centrifugal and centripetal forces, the structure of our earth itself, with it's* [sic] *distribution of lands, waters and atmosphere, animal and vegetable bodies, examined in all their minutest particles, insects mere atoms of life, yet as perfectly organised* [sic] *as man or mammoth, the mineral substances, their generation and uses, it is impossible, I say, for the human mind not to believe that there is, in all this, design, cause and effect, up to an ultimate cause, a fabricator of all things from matter and motion, their preserver and regulator while permitted to exist in their present forms, and their regenerator into new and other forms. we see, too, evident proofs of the necessity of a superintending power to maintain the Universe in it's* [sic] *course and order. stars, well known, have disappeared, new ones have come into view, comets, in their incalculable courses, may run foul of suns and planets and require renovation under other laws; certain races of animals are become extinct; and were there* *no restoring power, all existences might extinguish successively, one by one,* *until all should be reduced to a shapeless chaos. so irresistible are these* *evidences of an intelligent and powerful Agent that, of the infinite numbers* *of men who have existed thro' all time, they have believed, in the proportion* *of a million at least to Unit, in the hypothesis of an eternal pre-existence* *of a creator, rather than in that of a self-existent Universe. surely this* *unanimous sentiment renders this more probable than that of the few in the* *other hypothesis some early Christians indeed have believed in the coeternal* *pre-*existance [sic] *of both the Creator and the world, without changing* *their relation of cause & effect. that this was the opinion of St Thomas,* *we are informed by Cardinal Toleto, in these words* "Deus ab æterno fuit jam omnipotens, sicut cum produxit mundum. ab æterno potuit producere mundum.—si sol ab æterno esset, lumen an æterno esset; et si pes, similiter vestigium. at lumen et vestigium effectus sunt efficientis solis et pedis; potuit ergo cum causâ æterna effectus coæterna esse. cujus sententiæ est S. Thomas Theologorum primus." *Cardinal Toleta.*

Of the nature of this being we know nothing. Jesus tells us that "God is a *Spirit." 4. John 24. but without defining what a spirit is "πνευμα ὁ θεος."* *down to the 3ᵈ century we know that it was still deemed material; but of* *a lighter subtler matter than then our gross bodies. so says Origen.* "Deus igitur, cui anima similis est, juxta Originem, reapte corporalis est; sed graviorum tantum ratione corporum incorporeus." *these are the words of Huet in his commentary on Origen. Origen himself* *says* "appellatio ασοματον apud nostros scriptores est inusitata et incognita." *so also Tertullian* "quis autem negabit Deum esse corpus, etsi deus spiritus? spiritus etiam corporis sui generis, in suâ effigie." *Tertullian. these two fathers were of the 3ᵈ century. Calvin's* *character of this supreme being seems chiefly copied from that of the Jews.* *but the reformation of these blasphemous attributes, and substitution of* *those more worthy, pure and sublime, seems to have been the chief object of* *Jesus in his discources to the Jews: and his doctrine of the Cosmogony of* *the world is very clearly laid down in the 3 first verses of the 1ˢᵗ chapter of* *John, in these words,* "εν αρχη ην ὁ λογος, και ὁ λογος ην προς τον θεον και θεος ην ὁ λογος. οὑτος ην εν αρχη προς τον θεον. παντα δε αυτου εγενετο, και χωρις αυτου εγενετο ουδε ἑν ὁ γεγονεν." *which truly translated means* "*in the beginning God existed, and reason* [or mind] *was with God, and* *that mind was God. this was in the beginning with God. all things were*

*created by it, and without it was made not one thing which was made."
yet this text, so plainly declaring the doctrine of Jesus that the world was
created by the supreme, intelligent being, has been perverted by modern
Christians to build up a second person of their tritheism by a mistranslation
of the word λογος. one of it's* [sic] *legitimate meanings indeed is "a word."
but, in that sense, it makes an unmeaning jargon: while the other meaning
"reason," equally legitimate, explains rationally the eternal preexistence of
God, and his creation of the world. knowing how incomprehensible it was
that "a word," the mere action or articulation of the voice and organs of
speech could create a world, they undertake to make of this articulation a
second preexisting being, and ascribe to him, and not to God, the creation
of the universe. the Atheist here plumes himself on the uselessness of such a
God, and the simpler hypothesis of a self-existent universe. the truth is that
the greatest enemies to the doctrines of Jesus are those calling themselves the
expositors of them, who have perverted them for the structure of a system
of fancy absolutely incomprehensible, and without any foundation in his
genuine words. and the day will come when the mystical generation of
Jesus, by the supreme being as his father in the womb of a virgin will be
classed with the fable of the generation of Minerva in the brain of Jupiter.
but we may hope that the dawn of reason and freedom of thought in these
United States will do away all this artificial scaffolding, and restore to us
the primitive and genuine doctrines of this the most venerated reformer of
human errors.*

*So much for your quotation of Calvin's "mon dieu! jusqu'a quand"
in which, when addressed to the God of Jesus, and our God, I join you
cordially, and await his time and will with more readiness than reluctance.
may we meet there again, in Congress, with our antient Colleagues, and
receive with them the seal of approbation "Well done, good and faithful
servants."*
Th: Jefferson

To James Smith (on Unitarianism):

Monticello Dec. 8. 22.
Sir
*I have to thank you for your pamphlets on the subject of Unitarianism,
and to express my gratification with your efforts for the revival of primitive
Christianity in your quarter. no historical fact is better established than
that the doctrine of one god, pure and uncompounded was that of the*

early ages of Christianity; and was among the efficacious doctrines which gave it triumph over the polytheism of the antients [sic]*, sickened with the absurdities of their own theology. nor was the unity of the supreme being ousted from the Christian creed by the force of reason, but by the sword of civil government wielded at the will of the fanatic Athanasius. the hocus-pocus phantasm of a god like another Cerberus, with one body and three heads had it's* [sic] *birth and growth in the blood of thousands and thousands of martyrs. and a strong proof of the solidity of the primitive faith is it's* [sic] *restoration as soon as a nation arises which vindicates to itself the freedom of religious opinion, and it's* [sic] *eternal divorce from the civil authority. the pure and simple unity of the creator of the universe is now all but ascendant in the Eastern states; it is dawning in the West, and advancing towards the South; and I confidently expect that the present generation will see Unitarianism become the general religion of the United States. the Eastern presses are giving us many excellent pieces on the subject, and Priestly's learned writings on it are, or should be in every hand. in fact the Athanasian paradox that one is three, and three but one is so incomprehensible to the human mind that no candid man can say he has any idea of it, and how can he believe what presents no idea. he who thinks he does only decieves* [sic] *himself. he proves also that man, once surrendering his reason, has no remaining guard against absurdities the most monstrous, and like a ship without rudder is the sport of every wind. with such persons gullability* [sic] *which they call faith takes the helm from the hand of reason and the mind becomes a wreck.*
I write with freedom, because, while I claim a right to believe in one god, if so my reason tells me, I yield as freely to others that of believing in three. both religions I find make honest men, & that is the only point society has any authority to look to—altho' this mutual freedom should produce mutual indulgence, yet I wish not to be brought in question before the public on this or any other subject, and I pray you to consider me as writing under that trust. I take no part in controversies religious or political. at the age of 80. tranquility is the greatest good of life, and the strongest of our desires that of dying in the good will of all mankind. and with the assurances of all my good will to Unitarian & Trinitarian, to whig & tory accept for yourself that of my entire respect.
Th: Jefferson

To Benjamin Rush (on Christianity):

Washington April 21. 1803.
Dear Sir
In some of the delightful conversations with you, in the evenings of 1798. 99. which served as an Anodyne to the afflictions of the crisis through which our country was then labouring, the Christian religion was sometimes our topic: and I then promised you that, one day or other, I would give you my views of it. they are the result of a life of enquiry & reflection, and very different from that Anti-Christian system, imputed to me by those who know nothing of my opinions. to the corruptions of Christianity, I am indeed opposed; but not to the genuine precepts of Jesus himself. I am a Christian, in the only sense in which he wished any one to be; sincerely attached to his doctrines, in preference to all others; ascribing to himself every human excellence, & believing he never claimed any other. at the short intervals, since these conversations, when I could justifiably abstract my mind from public affairs, this subject has been under my contemplation. but the more I considered it, the more it expanded beyond the measure of either my time or information. in the moment of my late departure from Monticello, I recieved [sic] from Doctr [sic]. Priestly his little treatise of "Socrates & Jesus compared." this being a section of the general view I had taken of the field, it became a subject of reflection, while on the road, and unoccupied otherwise. the result was, to arrange in my mind a Syllabus, or Outline, of such an Estimate of the comparative merits of Christianity, as I wished to see executed, by some one of more leisure and information for the task than myself. this I now send you, as the only discharge of my promise I can probably ever execute. and, in confiding it to you, I know it will not be exposed to the malignant perversions of those who make every word from me a text for new misrepresentations & calumnies. I am moreover averse to the communication of my religious tenets to the public; because it would countenance the presumption of those who have endeavored to draw them before that tribunal, and to seduce public opinion to erect itself into that Inquisition over the rights of conscience, which the laws have so justly proscribed. it behoves every man, who values liberty of conscience for himself, to resist invasions of it in the case of others; or their case may, by change of circumstances, become his own. it behoves him too, in his own case, to give no example of concession, betraying the common right of independant opinion, by answering questions of faith, which the laws have left between god & himself. Accept my affectionate salutations.
Th: Jefferson

RELATED PLACES OF INTEREST

*T*hese historic locations related to this book can be found in the city of Fredericksburg:

Thomas Jefferson Religious Freedom Monument

Washington Avenue Mall at Pitt Street, Fredericksburg, VA 22401

This monument commemorates the Virginia Statute for Religious Freedom. The stones for the monument were taken from churches throughout the country. It is the site of the Religious Freedom Day celebration.

Kenmore Plantation

1201 Washington Avenue, Fredericksburg, VA 22401

Built in the 1770s, this was the home of Fielding and Betty Washington Lewis and is the only surviving structure from the 1,300-acre Kenmore Plantation.

The building now sitting on the Weedon Tavern site. *Dawn Bowen, HMdb.org.*

CHATHAM MANOR

120 CHATHAM LANE, FREDERICKSBURG, VA 22405

For more than a century, this was the center of a large, thriving plantation and the only private residence in the United States to be visited by George Washington, Thomas Jefferson, Abraham Lincoln and Dwight D. Eisenhower.

FERRY FARM

268 KINGS HIGHWAY, FREDERICKSBURG, VA 22405

Ferry Farm, also known as the George Washington Boyhood Home, is the farm and home where George Washington spent much of his childhood.

John Paul Jones House

501 Caroline Street, Fredericksburg, VA 22401

This is the only house in America that naval hero John Paul Jones called home. The house was owned by his older brother William Paul, who used it for his tailoring business.

James Monroe Museum

908 Charles Street, Fredericksburg, VA 22401

This museum holds the country's largest collection of memorabilia related to James Monroe, the fifth president of the United States.

Mary Washington House

1200 Charles Street, Fredericksburg, VA 22401

This is the house in which George Washington's mother, Mary Ball Washington, resided toward the end of her life.

Hugh Mercer Apothecary Shop

1020 Caroline Street, Fredericksburg, VA 22401

Hugh Mercer Apothecary was a pharmacy founded by Hugh Mercer in the mid-eighteenth century. Mercer was a doctor who fled Scotland after the Battle of Culloden.

Fredericksburg Masonic Cemetery

998 Charles Street, Fredericksburg, VA 22401

The land for the Masonic Cemetery was donated to the local lodge in 1784 by James Somerville, a Scottish merchant and early mayor of Fredericksburg.

Lewis Store

1200 Caroline Street, Fredericksburg, VA 22401

The Lewis Store, also known as the Fielding Lewis Store, is a historic commercial building. It was built by John Lewis and operated by him and his son, Fielding Lewis, who was married to George Washington's sister.

Old Stone Warehouse

923 Sophia Street, Fredericksburg, VA 22401

The warehouse, built circa 1813, was built by businessman and patriot Thomas Goodwin. The current building was constructed on top of an old tobacco warehouse from 1754 that had been destroyed by a fire in 1807.

Rising Sun Tavern

1304 Caroline Street, Fredericksburg, VA 22401

Built by George Washington's youngest brother, Charles, around 1760 as his home, this frame building became a tavern in 1792, when it was purchased by the Wallace family.

St. George's Episcopal Church

905 Princess Anne Street, Fredericksburg, VA 22401

For nearly three hundred years, St. George's has been the sole Episcopal church in downtown Fredericksburg. It was targeted by federal artillery and sustained damage during the Battle of Fredericksburg in 1862.

Fredericksburg Visitor Center

706 Caroline Street, Fredericksburg, VA 22401

The visitor center offers comprehensive touring information. Maps, brochures, information on tour services and special event tickets are available. Local souvenirs are also available for purchase.

BIBLIOGRAPHY

A Bicentennial Project. Alexandria, VA: Thomas Jefferson Institute, 1976.

Buckley, Thomas E. *Establishing Religious Freedom: Jefferson's Statute in Virginia.* Illustrated edition. Charlottesville: University of Virginia Press, 2019.

Cummings, John F. *Fredericksburg and Spotsylvania Through Time.* Charleston, SC: America Through Time, 2017.

Davidson, Butler. *Jefferson.* Boston, MA: New Word City, 2018.

Davies, Lawrence A. *Proclamation: Religious Freedom Day.* Fredericksburg, VA: Free Lance-Star, 1996.

Ellis, Joseph J. *American Sphinx: The Character of Thomas Jefferson.* New York: Vintage Books, 1998.

Ferling, John. *Adams and Jefferson: The Tumultuous Election of 1800.* Oxford, UK: Oxford University Press, 2004.

Free Lance-Star. "Freedom Medals Soon Go on Sale." December 10, 1985.

Gordon-Reed, Annette. *The Hemings of Monticello: An American Family.* Reprint, New York: W.W. Norton & Company, 2009.

———. *Thomas Jefferson and Sally Hemings: An American Controversy.* Updated edition, Charlottesville: University of Virginia Press, 1998.

Gordon-Reed, Annette, and Peter S. Onuf. *"Most Blessed of the Patriarchs": Thomas Jefferson and the Empire of the Imagination.* Reprint, New York: Liveright, 2017.

Harris, James F. *The Serpentine Wall: The Winding Boundary Between Church and State in the United States.* London: Routledge, 2017.

Howe, Bill. "Forefathers Would Wonder What Went Wrong." *Free Lance-Star*, May 14, 1994.

Hyland, William G., Jr. *Thomas Jefferson: The Sally Hemings Sex Scandal.* New York: Thomas Dunne Books, 2009.

Jamison, John A. "Address: Religious Freedom Day." January 13, 1982.

Jefferson, Thomas. *Autobiography of Thomas Jefferson*. Scott's Valley, CA: CreateSpace Independent Publishing Platform, 2017.

———. *The Life and Selected Writings of Thomas Jefferson*. Reprint, New York: Modern Library, 1998.

———. *The Quotable Jefferson*. Edited by John P. Kaminski. Princeton, NJ: Princeton University Press, 2006.

———. *Thomas Jefferson: Travels: Selected Writings, 1784–1789*. Edited by Anthony Brandt. Washington, D.C.: National Geographic, 2006.

Kent, Toby. *Fredericksburg (Then and Now)*. Illustrated edition. Charleston, SC: Arcadia Publishing, 2010.

Kilmeade, Brian, and Don Yaeger. *Thomas Jefferson and the Tripoli Pirates: The Forgotten War That Changed American History*. New York: Sentinel, 2015.

Kranish, Michael. *Flight From Monticello: Thomas Jefferson at War*. Oxford, UK: Oxford University Press, 2010.

Meacham, Jon. *Thomas Jefferson: The Art of Power*. New York: Random House, 2013.

Monticello staff. *Thomas Jefferson's Monticello*. 2nd ed. Charlottesville, VA: Thomas Jefferson Foundation Inc., 2019.

Peterson, Merrill D., and Robert C. Vaughan, eds. *The Virginia Statute for Religious Freedom: Its Evolution and Consequences in American History*. Cambridge: Cambridge University Press, 1988.

Peterson, Merrill I. "Jefferson and Religious Freedom." *Atlantic Monthly*, December 1994.

Pullen, Rick. "The Freedom to Worship." *Free Lance-Star*, July 29, 1982.

Strobel, Jennifer. "Statute a Godsend, Students Say." *Free Lance-Star*, January 17, 1986.

Taylor, Alan. *Thomas Jefferson's Education*. Illustrated edition. New York: W.W. Norton & Company, 2019.

Wills, Garry. *Negro President: Jefferson and the Slave Power*. Boston, MA: Mariner Books, 2005.

Websites

California Family Counsel. "Never Take Religious Freedom for Granted." https://www.californiafamily.org/2022/01/never-take-religious-freedom-for-granted/.

Encyclopedia Virginia. "Virginia Statute for Establishing Religious Freedom (1786)." https://encyclopediavirginia.org/entries/virginia-statute-for-establishing-religious-freedom-1786/.

Historical Marker Database. "Weedon's Tavern, The City of Fredericksburg, Virginia." https://www.hmdb.org/m.asp?m=1060.

History on the Net. "Thomas Jefferson, Religious Freedom, and the First
   Amendment." https://www.historyonthenet.com/thomas-jefferson-religious-
   freedom-and-the-first-amendment.
Monticello. "Thomas Jefferson Encyclopedia." https://www.monticello.org/.
National Archives. "A Bill for Establishing Religious Freedom, 18 June 1779."
   https://founders.archives.gov/documents/Jefferson/01-02-02-0132-0004-0082.
————. "Thomas Jefferson Papers." Founders Online. https://founders.
   archives.gov/?q=%20Author%3A%22Jefferson%2C%20Thomas
   %22&s=1111211111&r=1.
National Park Service. "Thomas Jefferson at Chatham—Fredericksburg." https://
   www.nps.gov/frsp/learn/historyculture/jeff.htm.
Revolutionary War Journal. "Colonel Weedon's Tavern: American Revolution Patriots'
   Favorite Hangout." https://www.revolutionarywarjournal.com/weedons-tavern/.
University of Mary Washington. "Draft for a Bill to Establish Religious Freedom
   in Virginia (1779)." https://cas.umw.edu/cprd/files/2011/09/Jefferson-
   Statute-2-versions.pdf.

Letters (In Order of Appearance)

National Archives. "From Thomas Jefferson to Charles Lewis Bankhead, 27
   February 1809." Founders Online. https://founders.archives.gov/documents/
   Jefferson/99-01-02-9907.
————. "From Thomas Jefferson to Mann Page, 8 December 1793." Founders
   Online. https://founders.archives.gov/documents/Jefferson/01-27-02-0467.
————. "From Thomas Jefferson to Hartman Elliot, 15 February 1794." Founders
   Online. https://founders.archives.gov/documents/Jefferson/01-28-02-0022.
————. "From Thomas Jefferson to Mary Jefferson Eppes, [6 June 1798]." Founders
   Online. https://founders.archives.gov/documents/Jefferson/01-30-02-0281.
————. "From Thomas Jefferson to Thomas Mann Randolph, 7 June 1798." Founders
   Online. https://founders.archives.gov/documents/Jefferson/01-30-02-0285.
————. "From Thomas Jefferson to Martha Jefferson Randolph, 27 December
   1798." Founders Online. https://founders.archives.gov/documents/
   Jefferson/01-30-02-0413.
————. "From Thomas Jefferson to Robert Lewis, 10 November 1824." Founders
   Online. https://founders.archives.gov/documents/Jefferson/98-01-02-4677.
————. "From Thomas Jefferson to John Hankart, 28 June 1803." Founders Online.
   https://founders.archives.gov/documents/Jefferson/01-40-02-0472.
————. "From Thomas Jefferson to William H. Cabell, 31 July 1807." Founders
   Online. https://founders.archives.gov/documents/Jefferson/99-01-02-6075.
————. "From Thomas Jefferson to George Weedon, 12 January 1781." Founders
   Online. https://founders.archives.gov/documents/Jefferson/01-04-02-0424.

———. "From Thomas Jefferson to George Weedon, 21 January 1781." Founders Online. https://founders.archives.gov/documents/Jefferson/01-04-02-0527.

———. "From Thomas Jefferson to George Weedon, 31 January 1781." Founders Online. https://founders.archives.gov/documents/Jefferson/01-04-02-0603.

———. "Thomas Jefferson to Miles King, 26 September 1814." Founders Online. https://founders.archives.gov/documents/Jefferson/03-07-02-0495.

———. "Thomas Jefferson to Charles Thomson, 9 January 1816." Founders Online. https://founders.archives.gov/documents/Jefferson/03-09-02-0216.

———. "From Thomas Jefferson to Benjamin Rush, 21 April 1803." Founders Online. https://founders.archives.gov/documents/Jefferson/01-40-02-0178-0001.

———. "From Thomas Jefferson to Peter Carr, with Enclosure, 10 August 1787." Founders Online. https://founders.archives.gov/documents/Jefferson/01-12-02-0021.

———. "V. To the Danbury Baptist Association, 1 January 1802." Founders Online. https://founders.archives.gov/documents/Jefferson/01-36-02-0152-0006.

———. "Thomas Jefferson to Richard Rush, 31 May 1813." Founders Online. https://founders.archives.gov/documents/Jefferson/03-06-02-0155.

———. "Thomas Jefferson to Miles King, 26 September 1814." Founders Online. https://founders.archives.gov/documents/Jefferson/03-07-02-0495.

———. "Thomas Jefferson to Charles Thomson, 9 January 1816." Founders Online. https://founders.archives.gov/documents/Jefferson/03-09-02-0216.

———. "Thomas Jefferson to Timothy Pickering, 27 February 1821." Founders Online. https://founders.archives.gov/documents/Jefferson/03-16-02-0548.

———. "From Thomas Jefferson to Thomas Whittemore, 5 June 1822." Founders Online. https://founders.archives.gov/documents/Jefferson/98-01-02-2850.

———. "From Thomas Jefferson to John Adams, 11 April 1823." Founders Online. https://founders.archives.gov/documents/Jefferson/98-01-02-3446.

———. "To James Madison from Thomas Jefferson, 16 December 1786." Founders Online. https://founders.archives.gov/documents/Madison/01-09-02-0108.

———. "From Thomas Jefferson to George Wythe, 13 August 1786." Founders Online. https://founders.archives.gov/documents/Jefferson/01-10-02-0162.

———. "Thomas Jefferson to Jacob De La Motta, 1 September 1820." Founders Online. https://founders.archives.gov/documents/Jefferson/03-16-02-0184.

———. "From Thomas Jefferson to George Outlaw, 24 June 1806." Founders Online. https://founders.archives.gov/documents/Jefferson/99-01-02-3895.

———. "Thomas Jefferson and George Wythe to Benjamin Harrison, 18 June 1779." Founders Online. https://founders.archives.gov/documents/Jefferson/01-02-02-0131.

———. "Thomas Jefferson to Francis Adrian Van der Kemp, 25 April 1816." Founders Online. https://founders.archives.gov/documents/Jefferson/03-09-02-0473.

————. "From Thomas Jefferson to John Adams, 11 April 1823." Founders Online. https://founders.archives.gov/documents/Jefferson/98-01-02-3446.

————. "From Thomas Jefferson to James Smith, 8 December 1822." Founders Online. https://founders.archives.gov/documents/Jefferson/98-01-02-3202.

————. "From Thomas Jefferson to Benjamin Rush, 21 April 1803." Founders Online. https://founders.archives.gov/documents/Jefferson/01-40-02-0178-0001.

INDEX

ABOUT THE AUTHOR

M ichael Aubrecht is an experienced author, historian and producer with a genuine passion for preserving and presenting the past through film and the written word in a way that engages individuals and instills an interest in them to explore the subject further on their own. He lives in historic Fredericksburg, Virginia, surrounded by eighteenth- and nineteenth-century historical sites. Michael has written multiple books, including *Historic Churches of Fredericksburg: Houses of the Holy* and *The Civil War in Spotsylvania: Confederate Campfires at the Crossroads*. He has published many articles for print and online magazines, including *Patriots of the American Revolution* and *Emerging Civil War*. Michael produced the documentary *The Angel of Marye's Heights*, hosts the YouTube series *The Naked Historian* and manages the Facebook page Today's History Lesson. He is the founder of the Jefferson Project. Michael has lectured at many venues such as the Manassas Museum and the University of Mary Washington. He was the cochair of the National Civil War Life Foundation and personal copy writer for renowned Civil War artist Mort Kunstler. By day, Michael is a technical writer and video producer for Lockheed Martin. He credits his wife, Tracy; children, Dylan, Madison, Kierstyn and Jackson; and grandson, Eli, with inspiring him as a writer. Visit Michael online at www.michaelaubrecht.wordpress.com.

OTHER BOOKS
BY MICHAEL AUBRECHT
Published by The History Press

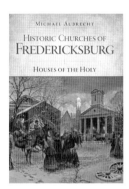

Historic Churches of Fredericksburg: Houses of the Holy

Historic Churches of Fredericksburg: Houses of the Holy recalls stories of rebellion, racism and reconstruction as experienced by Secessionists, Unionists and the African American population in Fredericksburg's landmark churches during the Civil War and Reconstruction eras. Using a wide variety of materials compiled from the local National Park archives, author Michael Aubrecht presents multiple perspectives from local believers and nonbelievers who witnessed the country's Great Divide. Learn about the importance of faith in old Fredericksburg through the recollections of local clergy such as Reverend Tucker Lacy; excerpts from enslaved persons' narratives as recorded by Joseph F. Walker; impressions of military commanders such as Robert E. Lee and Stonewall Jackson; and stories of the conflict over African American churches.

The Civil War in Spotsylvania County:
Confederate Campfires at the Crossroads

From 1861 to 1865, hundreds of thousands of troops from both sides of the Civil War marched through, battled and camped in the woods and fields of Spotsylvania County, earning it the nickname "Crossroads of the Civil War." When not engaged with the enemy or drilling, a different kind of battle occupied soldiers' boredom, hunger, disease, homesickness, harsh winters and spirits both broken and swigged. Focusing specifically on the local Confederate encampments, renowned author and historian Michael Aubrecht draws from published memoirs, diaries, letters and testimonials from those who were there to give a fascinating new look into the day-to-day experiences of camp life in the Confederate army. So, huddle around the fire and discover the days when the only meal was a scrap of hardtack, temptation was mighty and a new game they called "baseball" passed the time when not playing poker or waging a snowball war on fellow compatriots.